Memoirs of an

Artist

**Confessions of a
Dangerous Mind**

Memoirs of an *Artist*

Confessions of a Dangerous Mind

Billy Selesnick

With a Prelude by
Chuck Barris

ABSOLUTELY AMAZING eBOOKS

ABSOLUTELY AMAZING eBOOKS

Published by Whiz Bang LLC, 926 Truman Avenue, Key West, Florida 33040, USA.

Memoirs of an Artist copyright © 2017 by Billy Selesnick. Electronic compilation / paperback edition copyright © 2017 by Whiz Bang LLC. Excerpt from *Confessions of a Dangerous Mind* copyright © 2002 Barris Industries.

All rights reserved. No part of this book may be reproduced, scanned, or transmitted in any form or by any means, electronic or mechanical, including photocopying, recording, or any information storage and retrieval system, without permission in writing from the publisher. Please do not participate in or encourage piracy of copyrighted materials in violation of the author's rights. Purchase only authorized ebook editions.

This work is based on factual events. However, many names, characters, places, and incidents either are the product of the author's imagination or are used fictitiously, and any resemblance to actual persons, living or dead, businesses, companies, events, or locales is entirely coincidental. While the author has made every effort to provide accurate information at the time of publication, neither the publisher nor the author assumes any responsibility for errors, or for changes that occur after publication. Further, the publisher does not have any control over and does not assume any responsibility for author or third-party websites or their contents. How the ebook displays on a given reader is beyond the publisher's control.

For information contact
Publisher@AbsolutelyAmazingEbooks.com

ISBN-13: 978-1945772436 (Absolutely Amazing Ebooks)
ISBN-10: 1945772433

Memoirs of an

Artist

**Confessions of a
Dangerous Mind**

Introduction

In the late '70s, right before I became Associate Publisher of Harper's Magazine, the company did a deal with television game show producer Chuck Barris to publish his first novel, *You and Me, Babe*. Surprisingly, it became a New York Times bestseller, launching his brief literary career.

A likeable huckster, Charles Hirsch Barris had created *The Dating Game* back in 1965; the next year he followed up his success with *The Newlywed Game*. These were followed by a spate of shows: *The Family Game, Dream Girl of 1968*, and *How's Your Mother-in-Law?* But by 1974 the last of his shows, *The Newlywed Game*, had been dropped.

Chuck Barris spent six months writing *You and Me, Babe*, the fictionalized story of his first marriage. After being turned down by over a dozen publishers, he finally paid Harper's Magazine Press $35,000 to publish it. Putting up an additional $100,000 for promotion, Barris helped the book sell some 750,000 copies.

By 1976, Chuck Barris had made a comeback with an oddball television variety program, *The Gong Show*. He hosted it himself, becoming a TV cult figure.

In the mid '80s he penned an "unauthorized autobiography" titled *Confessions of a Dangerous Mind*. In it, he wrote: "I have written pop songs, I have been a television producer. I am responsible for polluting the airwaves with mind-numbing puerile entertainment. In addition, I have murdered 33 human beings." He claimed to have been a CIA hitman.

According to Barris, he joined the CIA in the early '60s. As an agent, he says he infiltrated the Civil Rights

Movement, met with militant Muslims in Harlem, and was sent abroad to kill enemies of the United States, sometimes under cover of travel for his game shows.

As *Time* Magazine described Barris's autography: "Lying to tell the Truth."

Maybe that's where Barris and Billy Selesnick intersect.

In this memoir by the well-known artist, Selesnick recalls his meetings with Barris when both were pursuing their deadly sidelines. Names, places, dates.

Later on, when Barris's *Confession of a Dangerous Mind* was made into a Miramax movie starring Sam Rockwell, the actor and the movie's director, George Clooney, called on Selesnick at Barris's suggestion, studying him for traces of how a hitman might look and act.

Billy Selesnick tells all (well, almost all) in *Memoirs of an Artist,* the meandering story of his life. While outlining his artistic growth, his druggie lifestyle, and sexual peccadillos, Selesnick doesn't shy away from talking about his old pal Chuck and their common profession.

How much is true?

"I decided not to ask him what was true," George Clooney says of Chuck Barris's book. We'll afford Billy Selesnick the same courtesy.

- Shirrel Rhoades
former Associate Publisher,
Harper's Magazine

Prologue
By Chuck Barris

Actually, there's no need to detail my step-by-step indoctrination into the Central Intelligence Agency. Suffice it to say that I passed all the testing and interviews. And, later, the FBI investigation and clearance. And, still later, my intelligence education in Washington, Langley, and on the "farm," our nickname for the Company's advanced training center. I did surprisingly well, performing gallantly and taking to "spooking" with a zest and proficiency unmatched by most of my classmates. I was a straight A student in operational methods and the execution of clandestine affairs. When it came time to pick a major, I decided on Counter Intelligence.

"Don't forget," said our instructor, poised to move his pointer across an information-packed blackboard, "the Foreign Intelligence staff is concerned with information-*collection* operations; the Psychological Warfare and Paramilitary staffs with *action* operations; and the Counter Intelligence staff with the *protection* of Foreign, Psychological Warfare, and Paramilitary operations. The difference between action and collection operations is that an action operation *always* has a visible effect, whereas *neither* Counter Intelligence nor collection operations should *ever* have a visible effect.

No visible effect. Spooks.

~ ~ ~

Memoirs of an Artist

The knowledge that I was in line as a hit man excited the hell out of me. I was finally doing something adventurous. And patriotic. And *meaningful*.

Chapter One

In 1951 Ethel and Julius Rosenberg were sentenced to death and were executed in 1953. Harry Trumanwas President. Seoul, Korea fell to the communists. Japan signed the Peace Treaty in San Francisco. Libya gained independence from Italy. And most importantly, at five thirty-two in the morning on July 18th, I, Billy Selesnick was born in Mercer Hospital in Trenton, New Jersey.

Trenton was first settled in 1679 by Quakers who were being persecuted in England. They were an offshoot of the Protestants. They were a religious sect who were pacifists and shunned many of the luxurious things in life. They refused to take oaths, they were opposed to slavery, and they did not drink. They viewed themselves as Christians. In its earliest time many women took leadership roles.

In 1719 the town adapted the name Trent-town after William Trent, one of its leading landowners. The name later was shortened to Trenton.

During the Revolutionary war in 1776 the Battle of Trenton was fought there. History tells us that George Washington left his encampment (which was on the Pennsylvania side of the Delaware River ten miles south of Trenton) at night, in a blizzard. It was Christmas Eve. He crossed the Delaware River with 2400 soldiers. There were 3000 more soldiers who were supposed to participate but they failed to meet at the designated time.

The launched boats stretched nine miles to the south along the Delaware. They all departed around the same time. They marched parallel to the river in a line with foot soldiers, mounted officers on horseback and cannons pulled by horses. The caravan proceeded in the cold, windy blizzard. They traveled over ten miles to Trenton. Many of the men had no shoes and had rags wrapped around their feet.

They made a surprise attack. in the morning on the Hessians at the enemy's barrack.

The Hessians were mercenaries who fought for the British. Four American soldiers were lost. One had died of frostbite during the march. The other three were shot during the battle. The Hessians were all asleep because they were drinking heavily the night before, celebrating Christmas. It was considered a great victory for the Americans and proved to be a pivotal battle in the Revolutionary war.

"Washington Crossing the Delaware" is depicted in a painting done in 1851. It is an oil-on-canvas by German American artist Emmanuelle Gottleib Leutze. It commemorated Washington crossing the Delaware on the night of December 25th during the Revolutionary war. Leutze's second version hangs at the Metropolitan Museum of Art in New York City.

Its first version was destroyed in a fire where it hung in a museum in Germany. There is also a copy in the White House. The painting depicts General George Washington in his long boats crossing the Delaware. Ice and snow were all around him. Its light captures the feel and the coldness of the occasion.

Trenton was a river town that had industries that ranged from pottery, laceworks and wire rope mills. Trenton became the State Capitol in 1790. Throughout the nineteenth century Trenton grew steadily as Europeans came to work in the many industries. Other nationally known industries were established from Champale beer to oyster crackers.

On one of the bridges crossing the Delaware there is a sign seen day and night that says

Billy Selesnick

"Trenton Makes the World Takes."

My father worked in the family dry cleaning business. He was born in 1927 in Trenton and grew up in the Depression. He remembers having shoes with holes on their soles. He would walk a mile to school, often in the snow in those shoes.

I remember stories which took place during the Depression about my grandmother's sister making bathtub gin. From one bathtub you could make a four-dollar profit. Their family all had emigrated from Eastern Europe around the turn of the century.

My mother was raised on a dairy farm outside of Trenton. Her father Charlie emigrated from Russia along with his brothers. They settled in Mount Holly, New Jersey. They started dairy farms with loans from a Jewish agency. They all became successful dairy farmers.

My parents met at a party in the late 1940's. They were married a few years before I was born. I would classify them as lower middle class liberals. Both of my parents were Jewish. We lived in a mixed neighborhood and my parents had many non-Jewish friends.

My sister was born a few years later. Her name was Mindy Sue. We lived in an area of Trenton known as The Island. It was close to the Delaware River. On the other side of the River was Pennsylvania. I would walk around the block from my house and take in the majestic view of the Delaware River.

In 1955 during the summer in Trenton three hurricanes hit back to back. The banks of the Delaware River overflowed its banks and high tide reached the Delaware canal several blocks away. It was considered one of the worst floods of the century. It was then we moved to higher ground on the other side of the canal. I remember seeing the River rise and we were rescued by boat and taken to higher land. The day we went back to check our house my father opened the door and all kinds of water and mud rushed out.

My father and his next-door neighbor took me and his friend's son swimming in the Delaware. We would have to walk through rapids and get to an island where there was a sandy beach and a monkey swing. I was scared when we walked through those rapids. The other kid that was with us was not scared at all. I remember being called a sissy.

I remember when I was little, all the socializing went on in our backyards. The neighbors would come over and we would play at sports. My father and his friends and the other kids all said I threw a baseball like a girl. I was constantly teased and tormented about this. I remember being called a faggot. My father and his friends tried to help me overcome this embarrassing deformity to no avail. So my nickname was sissy, faggot and crybaby. My feet stuck out and I walked like a duck. My mother took me to a podiatrist and I had to wear corrective shoes. They were uncomfortable and I soon abandoned them. As a result, I did not excel at most sports. I learned early on finding other things to fill my time. I developed a passion for reading.

Many years later the Delaware River served as an inspiration for many of my paintings. After high school I decided to embark on a career as a fine artist and did oil paintings. At the turn of the century a painting movement began ten miles to the south in a town called New Hope, Pennsylvania. Painters began settling there and specialized in paintings of the Delaware River, the mills, and the canals in the area. They were called the New Hope Impressionists."

In 1956, at a family gathering, I remember hearing

about a war and Israel. It had to do with the Suez Canal and people had died there. It was being discussed at the dinner table. Emotions ran high at Shabbos dinners at my grandmother's on Friday night.

For what I lacked in sports I made up for in other ways. I had a gift for memory. I remember the day Albert Einstein died. It was on the front page of the paper. I remember my father saying he was the smartest Jew in the world.

My mother was very sensitive about being Jewish. My father was from the city where it was more diverse. My mother was a country girl who grew up on a dairy farm. My grandmother Fay could feed a dinner party of eight on a dollar. First she would boil a chicken with an onion and few pieces of carrots and celery. The appetizer was chicken soup. With the chicken liver she would make chopped liver. The chicken was the main course for everyone. That's how it was in those days.

My grandfather was in the dry-cleaning business. After the end of World War II my father worked for his father in the summer when business was slow. My father also did construction work.

I was an average child who cried easily and did not do well at sports. I also ran away from fights. I attended a racially mixed public school from first through fourth grade.

On Sundays I went to synagogue for Sunday School. I loved Sunday School. I had a passion for the stories of the Old Testament. The books which we studied in Sunday School class had illustrations of Biblical stories, which captured my imagination, and I would try copying them with pencil and paper. I had dreams of becoming a rabbi.

Our parents were not satisfied with the education we were getting at public school. They also were not happy with the racial strife that was occurring there. I would carpool with other kids from the neighborhood. It was then I had exposure to other religions and philosophies.

In fifth grade I was accepted into a private Quaker school called Newtown Friends. The school was located a few miles from the river in Pennsylvania in a Quaker community called Newtown. A group of other kids from my neighborhood were accepted at the same time.

We had Quaker meetings on Wednesday morning. Meetings were the Quaker way of having a religious service. That usually entailed our assembly sitting in silence. A few of the elders or teachers would sit in front of the group. Sometimes if something moved people they would stand up and talk. This was seen as being moved by God. Our branch of Quakers did not sing or have a more regimented service. These Quaker meetings usually lasted forty-five minutes.

They lead simple lives, shunned luxury items and did not believe very much in new technology. In our area, where there were a lot of Quakers, many were farmers or teachers. They were also tolerant of other religions.

They taught us the fundamentals of the Quaker philosophy at school. They were by and large against the war in Vietnam. The Quakers were usually pacifists and anti war.

For me school was a place to socialize, and make friends. I was a daydreamer and the class clown, not showing much interest in studies. I was a very average child. In school, my priorities were to get attention from girls and to make them laugh.

I did have a passion for reading. I loved Greek myths and Roman history. In Newtown Friends, Latin was taught in sixth grade. The academics were more advanced than the education you would get in public school.

I also developed a love of art that year. It was probably 1965. I already had been copying illustrations of biblical stories out of my Sunday school books.

When I started at Newtown Friends, I began to illustrate some of my reports that I did in school. I was given an assignment to do a report on Mexico. I read books on Mexican art, specifically Diego Rivera. I used him as a model and source of inspiration when I had to illustrate my written report. The teacher said the drawings were good.

This is about the time that I decided I wanted to be an artist. I found an advertisement in a magazine that said, "Draw this pirate and send it in for a critique." The pirate was a sketch that was part of the advertisement. I drew that pirate and this girl who was in my class said it was really good. I never sent it in for the critique but that was the beginning for me. When drawing was part of an assignment in school, the teachers would say I had an aptitude for that subject. I also found that being able to draw pictures well would attract the attention of the girls in my class.

I also continued to have a passion for Bible stories. I had been going to Sunday School for years. I remember when I was in class one Sunday, I asked a question about a Bible story. I asked the Sunday school teacher what was sodomy. It came up when we were discussing Sodom and Gomorrah. The teacher said it was when two men had sex. And that one was being forced.

When my mother picked me up from Sunday School she said well, what have you learned in Sunday school today? I said I learned what Sodomy was. My mother asked, Well, what is it? I said when a man was being raped by another man. My mother was so pissed she called the Sunday School teacher and complained (she did not even know what sodomy was).

In fifth grade I began Hebrew studies after school and on weekends. I enjoyed the study of Hebrew. I particularly liked to draw Hebrew letters. I advanced from fifth to sixth grade without any problems. I achieved average grades with my classes.

In sixth grade I turned thirteen. I had my Bar Mitzvah at the local synagogue in Trenton. A Bar Mitzvah is when a thirteen-year-old is considered a man and he becomes a full member of his congregation. My Bar Mitzvah ceremony was the culmination of several years of study. At my ceremony the community was invited as well as friends and family. I was given a Torah portion, which was a section of the Torah, which I read in front of the congregation. That was a big thing for me. My parents were not particularly religious. My father went to temple twice a year. My mother went more often. I liked it more then they did because it was a place to learn and read from the Jewish books. I began to wrestle with the meaning of these books. I enjoyed the subject matter more in religious school then I did in Newtown Friends.

I was also educated in religious school about the Holocaust. We learned that Adolf Hitler in the 1930's began his systematic executions of over six million Jews. We also became aware of our Jewishness and of the persecution of Jews that still went on around the world.

We were also educated about the state of affairs with Israel. We were taught that Israel against great odds became a state in 1948. My parents, as well as the other Jewish families in the area, gave money to Israel. I remember hearing about it every year when it was time to give. The more money you gave, the more status you had in the community. I heard that Jews stuck together. That may have been true, but I had plenty of non-Jewish friends and my parents did too.

I had always had a difficult relationship with my father. It got worse when I was in high school. The only thing my father and I had in common at that age was we both like to go skiing. I started when I was about six or seven years old. I used to go to this place in between Trenton and Lambertville. It was called Belle Mountain. The county owned it. It was a hill with a rope tow and fairly steep. When we first went there it was before the rope tow, and we used to climb it. From there we graduated to trips to the Poconos. They were bigger and had a higher elevation. They also had chair lifts. I remember my father and I would be the first ones there. If we left at three, and the area was open for another two hours, my father would make me sell my ticket to some one that was just arriving. He would always say he wanted me to learn the value of a buck.

On weekends we sometimes would go to big ski areas in Vermont like Mount Snow or Killington, or Mount Washington in New Hampshire. He often left me alone while he mingled with the female skiers.

I also remember hearing about a place called Jew-Town. It's where the first Jews settled in Trenton. On Sundays, at five in the morning, my father and his friends would go there for bagels, fresh out of the oven. For some reason that name bothered me. A "Jew," in our school, had a connotation of a shady character with a big nose that was going to trick you out of something. So Jew- town sounded like something a little rough.

My father was in the dry cleaning business. That was an industry that was dominated by wise guys. When my father became successful, the Mafia tried to take over his business. They sewed lipsticks inside the liners of coats and that ruined the whole load when they were being cleaned in tumblers and dryers. Also, when he picked up coats in Atlantic City, he had to ride in the back with a shotgun. His trucks had already been hijacked. I remember loud fighting from that time.

Large amounts of cash were kept in the freezer. Once, I remember my father taking me to this gun shop and plopping me down on the counter. My father was buying bullets and asked the gun salesmen where certain gangsters lived. I looked around the shop and saw a huge poster of a blowup of a certain gun.

I grew up around firearms. There was a gun cabinet in the house and rifles. When my father was not home I would steal .22 caliber bullets and shoot birds outside my window. Sometimes I would set up books in my room and would gage how many books a .22 caliber weapon could go through. Then we had a shooting range in our basement.

I never liked sports so when the other kids were at sporting events I would build and detonate bombs. My first bombs were made with these wooden matches that had white tips on the end. I think they were phosphorus tips. Those were the kind of matches where you cut off the wooden part and put the end that is the red part with the white tip in a small box. This trick took a few dozen boxes of matches. I would detonate it with fuses made from firecrackers.

I lowered my bomb by rope down a sewer that created quite an echo that could be heard for miles. At least one neighbor had a stroke from my hobby. He was a survivor of the concentration camps. He had posttraumatic shock syndrome.

Summers I would either go to camp or work in my father's dry cleaning plant. Camp was at the Jewish Community Center. Our counselor was a concentration camp survivor, a man with tattoos of numbers on his arm. He had a short fuse. Some other kids set off firecrackers and this guy David had to quit his job. He just freaked out from loud noises.

I had an average relationship with my sister. She also had some emotional problems. She was very sensitive. She would cry a lot in many situations. When she went to camp, she was the only girl you could see there crying. They took these home movies when we arrived and then they showed everyone at camp. I remember feeling embarrassed seeing pictures of Mindy Sue crying. She also wet her bed until she was ten years old.

Seventh grade was a bad year for me academically, but I was allowed to advance into eighth grade. In eighth grade I could not keep up with my studies and before Thanksgiving, I was withdrawn from Newtown Friends and my parents shipped me off to Bordentown Military Institute.

Military school was a place where rejects whose parents had a few shekels went. Usually, kids who were charged with various crimes had the option of either going to prison, or if you were lucky, you could go to military school. Their crimes ranged from homicide, rape, armed robbery, car jacking, and car theft, incest and drug arrests. It was run by a retired colonel from the United States military. He looked and acted the part. His wife was the school librarian and she never cut you any slack.

The teachers were people that were not qualified as teachers in the public school system. Many of these teachers had been run out of the teaching profession for rape and child abuse. The curriculum was so restricted you could not even read a book like Catcher in the Rye.

The teachers from Newtown Friends and my

parents felt I needed more discipline. When my parents asked me how I felt about going, I thought it would be cool to come home on holidays in a uniform. Someone told me that women were attracted to men in uniforms.

My first day there was, to say the least, unusual. Before I came, there was some stealing going on in my dormitory, and the cadets were forced to wake up early and stand at attention until someone confessed for the stealing. My first morning there, we had to get up one hour and a half before reveille and stand at attention. That went on for a few weeks until the culprit was caught.

Military school was a shock. I did not have behavior problems. I was just not interested in school. Most of the cadets there had disciplinary problems and were on the rough side. It was an adjustment. We marched with rifles, wore military uniforms, and lead a boot camp life style. I remained there the rest of eighth, ninth and a few months of tenth grade.

I had the nickname of Lamp Shade because the Nazis made lampshades with the skin of dead Jews. I mean everybody got it. Blacks, Italians or Irish. There were other Jewish kids there too. I hated being there. I performed below average in academics and sports. I was the subject of a lot of bullying. The other cadets found out early I did not like to fight. There was no art program there and they discouraged visual and performing arts.

For each infraction, you had to march. I acquired a record amount of marching hours. In tenth grade, after a few months, I was asked to leave the school. I walk funny as it is. Surfers call me goofy foot, which means my feet stick out. That made me march with a funny gait. I was always tormented for that. When I think about it, Military School gave me the tools for what happened later in my life. So, in 1967 I enrolled in Trenton High.

I remember hearing on television about the 1967 war, Israel against its Arab neighbors. Most Jews were proud, some were embarrassed about taking land even though it was for self-protection. Jerusalem was united. The thought brings tears. Even the majority of the Arab and Christian shop owners were happy. Now everybody could make real money.

In 1948 the United Nations voted to let Israel be a state. Jerusalem was to remain on the Jordanian side. The Wailing Wall, the Jews holiest site, was made into a latrine. Jews no longer had access. The Jews from the old city of Jerusalem where they always had been a majority had to move to the other side. The boundary between Israel and Jordan ran through neighborhoods.

That was an incredible time to witness. I remember all the teachers talking about it at school. A lot of Americans Jews and some non-Jews went to volunteer and fight.

By this time the ideas of the hippy culture were finding its way to our area. It started out with the Beatles phenomenon. I was hanging out with kids who were smoking weed and listening to rock and roll.

I was against the war in Vietnam, and supported the Civil Rights Movement which was lead by Doctor Martin Luther King. There were a few kids in Trenton High who were hip. Our high school was an integrated school with over three thousand students. It was located on a street that on one side was mostly working class Italians (Chambersburg) and on the other side the Afro American neighborhood. Racial tension ran high there. If you were on the wrong side of the street there could be racially motivated fights.

BILLY AT AGE 17

I tried to fit in there but I was considered a problem kid coming to a rough school from military school. I was smoking weed with a few like-minded friends. I found it to be a pleasant experience. At the same time it made you an outlaw and a member of a criminal group. All the users and dealers had their phones tapped and we were always under surveillance. It was a relaxing pastime that bonded the users into a sort of fraternity. The high from grass also made contemporary rock and roll music more easily understood. The songs from that era were full of secret meanings and symbols. The police said that our music made us more subversive because of the subliminal anti-establishment messages that were in the songs.

I had obsessions with the female students. I also developed a secret life. On the outside it seemed my relationships with girls were normal. I had relationships with average looking females. However, I had developed a passion for heavyset girls with Rubenesque type figures. I would cultivate relationships and fantasize about painting their curvaceous bodies. I kept it somewhat hidden from my family and friends.

Even though I was an anti-establishment hippy, I still read and studied the Old Testament regularly. I was most interested in the mystical aspect of the holy books. I was into rock music and weekends would go to rock concerts in New York and Philadelphia. My friends and I grew long hair. We smoked weed and some of us dropped acid. I read books about Timothy Leary. Timothy Leary was a psychologist and writer known for his advocacy of L.S.D. and Psilocybin. During this time, these drugs were legal. Leary conducted experiments at Harvard University under the Harvard Psilocybin Project. These studies produced useful data. He also wrote a book advocating the questioning of authority. But Doctor Timothy Leary and his associate Doctor Richard Albert were fired from Harvard University.

Timothy Leary believed that L.S.D. had a use in psychiatry. He coined the phrase "turn on, tune in, and drop out." In the mid-1960s, Timothy Leary rented a mansion in Millbrook, which was near Poughkeepsie, New York and also near Vassar College. He would always be in the papers because of scandals and drug busts that went on there.

Timothy Leary in the 1960's and 1970's was arrested twenty-nine times worldwide. In 1970, Timothy Leary was given a twenty-year sentence for drugs.

In September of that year he was sprung from prison. For a fee of twenty thousand dollars he was rescued by the Brotherhood of Eternal Love and the

Weathermen. They eventually smuggled him and his wife to Algeria. Eldridge Cleaver had his government in exile there. Cleaver was a founding member along with Huey Newton of the Black Panther Party.

Leary eventually returned to the United States. He was imprisoned again after Algeria. He was released by Jerry Brown on April 21st, 1976. Afterwards, he wrote books and lectured on counter culture ideas. He had a sizeable following thourghout his career, including me. Timothy Leary died on May 31, 1996. Richard Nixon called Timothy Leary the most dangerous man on the face of the earth.

I identified with him because I took LSD about six times. The outcomes were usually a burst of new ideas and creativity. I also believed in Doctor Leary's philosophy about space colonization and his ideas on the future. I saw Doctor Leary a few times at different rock festivals and be-ins, as well as at anti-war protests. I did get to meet him and shake his hand. His partner Richard Albert changed his name to Baba Ram Dass and wrote a popular culture book called "Be Here Now" which was a best seller. I kept that on my bookshelf next to my copy of the Jerusalem Bible.

It was at this time that I first dropped acid. I got a tab of it from a friend who hung out at a luncheonette where drug users would congregate. It was called Brown Dot acid. It was on a small piece of paper which you would eat. It was dispensed onto the paper in liquid form with a nose dropper. It was very pure and dispersed in Milligrams. I took my first hit around lunchtime while hanging out with a few friends. Within thirty minutes I began to feel the effect. I saw my reflection in the window of this restaurant. My hair changed in front of my eyes from an Afro to shoulder length Prince Valiant style hair. The ground was feeling wobbly under my feet. Minutes turned to hours.

Hours seemed to go by in seconds. Time itself was warped. The colors changed all around me becoming more vivid. I looked up at the clouds and they transposed into withering snakes. I felt with each step I took that I was sinking into the center of the earth. Communication with my friends changed to non-verbal psychic talking where we could read each other's minds. People were walking by me and staring. I was paranoid because I felt that my appearance had changed. I felt I needed a place to hide. I somehow made the short walk to my home. I went to my room and got in bed feeling that it was a safe place to wait until the symptoms wore off. Unbeknownst to my mother and sister who were home, my mind was heaving and expanding to earth shattering delusions and apocalyptic revelations of the world coming to an end and being restarted again.

We pissed our parents off and we did not want to go to Vietnam.

The only fun thing about school was meeting women and that usually caused fights with your competitors. I was considered disruptive after a fight with a bully over a girl. I was sent to the school psychiatrist several times. This rougher bigger kid whose father was an abusive alcoholic liked the same girl that I did. He would pass me in the hall in between Classes. It was after English that this mean bully would pass me. Time in the hallways was the best time in school; you saw the most people then. So I was not going to hide. For months he would walk by me then either push me or spit at me or try to smack me across the face. I took it for months. I was a walking time bomb. All this rage had built up in me and I was not going to take it anymore.

The day came. I was standing in the middle of the hall with my arms wrapped around my chest looking all defiant. We made eye contact. He tried to stare me down and I did not budge. Suddenly he lost all his phony bravado. He approached. I took my arms and hands and pushed him straight out from me.

A crowd of mostly black men and women surrounded us. We were inter- twined for a few long moments before some teachers broke up the fight and sent us to the school disciplinarian.

The other time, I was in English class. We all had to do a report on our hobbies. I played the bongo drums to Afro Cuban music. My favorite was Mongo Santamaria and I would play my bongos to "Watermelon Man." I performed this in class and for a finale did a loud minor bird call. The class erupted in applause. A teacher from another class came to check it out. I was given a c-plus for this report. I was upset. I confronted my teacher in front of the class and the next day she raised it to a b- minus. I was still pissed off. I again challenged her in front of the class.

This time she sent me to the school psychiatrist. His name was Doctor Butcher. He asked me to look at these inkblots and asked me to tell him what I saw. The result was a meeting with my mother and the doctor telling her I was a misfit and would probably end up in jail.

An appointment was made this time with a private psychologist. I was to go after school. His diagnosis was similar.

I performed poorly in the academic program and they transferred me to the vocational school. It was decided that I was to study auto mechanics. In that part of the school you had to bring protection money so people would leave you alone.

Actually this rough Italian kid whose father was in the mob, brought these bootleg record albums to school every day. I was forced, if I knew what was good for me, to buy these on a daily basis. It would be good for my health.

I was the only Jew in the vocational school, because most Jews in Trenton went on to college. I learned how to fix breaks in that auto mechanic class. To this day I can still do it. Most people thought I had a screw loose. When the kids my age asked me in auto mechanics what my hobby was I said reading the Old Testament. That sealed my fate and I was looked upon as an outcast and weirdo. Most of the action or fun in our school was the lunch period. That was where all the racially motivated fights took place. They were common.

I read in the paper that Benjamin Netanyahu, now Prime Minister of Israel, was brother to a hero who died at Entebbe in Uganda at that time. Many Jewish people were hijacked on an airplane and taken as prisoners to the airport there. He led the daring successful rescue attempt and lost his life in the process. His brother Benjamin was also a hero. I heard that he was selling furniture then in Philadelphia and I went there to shake his hand.

My father hated me identifying with the hippies. He made me report to the plant after school and work. I told him I wanted to go March with Martin Luther King for civil rights. He told me Doctor King was a communist. He said that I was a communist for going to antiwar protests. Finally, he threw me out of the house for not getting a haircut and having a pierced ear. He told me if he caught me smoking pot he was going to have me arrested. I moved in with my aunt who lived nearby. On the day he threw me out I told him my hero was Martin Luther King.

Martin Luther King lived from 1929 to 1968. He was an American clergymen activist and leader in the African American civil rights movement. He is best known for his role in the advancement of civil rights movement using non-violent disobedience. Martin Luther King has become a national icon in the history of progressivism. A Baptist minister, Martin Luther King became a civil rights activist early in his career. He led the 1955 Montgomery Alabama bus boycott and helped found the Southern Christian Leadership Conference in 1957 serving as its first president. Martin Luther King also helped organize the 1963 March on Washington D.C. where he delivered his "I Have a Dream" speech. There he established a reputation as one of the greatest orators in American History. He also established a reputation as a radical and became an object of investigation by the Federal Bureau of Investigation. The F.B.I. investigated him for ties to communism. They recorded his extra marital affairs and reported them to the government. In 1964 he received the Nobel Peace Prize. Martin Luther King was assassinated in 1968 in Memphis Tennessee. This caused rioting across the country. Many Jews marched with him

My other heroes, I told my father, were Abbie Hoffman and Lenny Bruce. He slapped me across the face.

Abbott Hoffman was born in November of 1936. He was cofounder of the Youth International Party (Yippies). Abbie was a political and social activist. He came to prominence in the 1960s and he continued practicing his activism in the 1970s and he remains a symbol of that era. He was one of the Chicago Seven, a group of anti war protestors who organized a series of rallies at the 1968 Chicago Democratic Convention. Rioting took place between the protestors and the police. The organizers were put on trial which garnered a lot of media attention. I think at the convention they nominated Abbie Hoffman's pet pig for president; his name was Pegasus.

One of my favorite books from that era was written by Abbie Hoffman and it was called *Revolution for the Hell of It*. It was one of the best counter culture books and funniest books that I have ever read. Then I saw him on the *Merv Griffin Show* with Virginia Graham. She represented the Republicans. I think he had on his American Flag shirt. They had to take out his shirt visually because it violated a law about using the flag as a shirt. It created a lot of controversy. Then he and some Yippies tried to levitate the Pentagon. That got a lot of media attention. The newspapers were playing right into it. They did that to protest the war in Vietnam. I was totally into it. For his next prank, he and a bunch of Yippies went to Wall Street where they went up to a balcony overlooking the trading floor. They then threw hundreds of dollars over the balcony to protest American greed and capitalism. Again they were on the front page of the paper. They really captured the attention of a lot of people.

He wrote another bestseller called *Steal this Book*. Both of his books became a sort of bible for me. Then Abbie Hoffmann was either set up or was involved with selling cocaine in Greenwich Village. Rather than go to jail he went underground for several years. He was living near the Saint Lawrence River under an assumed name and was an environmental activist. He eventually turned himself in. He did a reduced sentence of several months.

When he got out he wrote, lectured and eventually moved to New Hope, Pa. There was a protest there. It was called Dump the Pump. About 15 miles north of New Hope there was a pumping station that was diverting water from the Delaware to cool down some type of nuclear plant. Abbie Hoffman was very involved in organizing and taking part in that protest.

They eventually won their case. The continued operation of this pump would have upset the eco levels for the fish and wild life in that area.

Abbie Hoffmann died from an accidental drug overdose in 1998. That happened in New Hope, Pennsylvania, at a friend of mine's house. I was lucky enough to get to know him personally at that time. I was under negotiations with him at the time of his death for the right to do a portrait of him. Some letters had gone back and forth between us on the matter.

Leonard Alfred Schneider was born October 3 1925. He was better known by his stage name Lenny Bruce. He was an American standup comedian, social critic and satirist. He was known for his open free- style and dangerous and critical form of comedy which integrated politics, religion and sex.

His wild personal life was marked by rampant drug use and promiscuity. He was a compelling figure. He died from an accidental drug overdose August 3, 1966.

My first wife, Cindy, had an Aunt Joan who was a girlfriend of Lenny Bruce. She lived with him for several years. Cindy and I visited Aunt Joan before she died in Los Angeles.

She gave us photos that she took of him as well as letters. She died still being in love with him.

Several months later after living as a hippy at my aunt's, my father asked me to come back. One of his conditions was that we all see a psychiatrist. My sister was having problems too. She looked up to me and did what I did.

In 1968 when Martin Luther King was assassinated, rioting started at Trenton High. They let us out of school early. The police and the T.V. cameras were there. It was basically black against white.

The fights would happen either in the lunchroom, the hallways, and the area outside the school. On that day the fighting started outside the school. A group of whites mostly Italians approached a group of Afro Americans. Car antennas were ripped off of cars and they were used as swords. Several students had puncture wounds from the tips of the antennas. Forty kids were put in the hospital that day.

The hippies were on the black side philosophically but mob ruled and sometimes the white hippies could be attacked by black mobs.

The rioting spread to downtown Trenton that night. It was reported that Black Panthers were in town helping to create chaos. There were many fires for several nights, as well as snipers. The National Guard was called in. School was closed for two weeks. Several people had been killed.

The Black Panthers were founded by Huey Newton in 1966 in Oakland California. They were an African American Revolutionary Socialist Party that ended in 1982. They believed in Black Nationalism and they were anti- capitalist, anti-drug, anti-racism, anti-fascism and anti-imperialism. They were Marxist and Leninist, Maoist and anti-Zionist. I read about them and supported a lot of their platform but disagreed with their stance on Israel.

My father's plant was in a black neighborhood. There were threats of firebombs and he had armed security guards in his business. The arsenal of shot guns, pistols, and rifles were left on the counters so looters could see them. My father's plant also got hundreds of bomb threats.

On one hand, in our white neighborhood, we were worried that blacks would come in and start trouble. On the other hand, my father had over one hundred Afro-American workers. I was close to them, having practically grown up in the plant.

I liked the black panthers and the leaders of the antiwar movement. They were my heroes. I especially liked the Yippies and the people that were called the Chicago 7. They were charged for starting riots at the Democratic Convention in Chicago in 1968.

It was my plan if anything happened to my parents that I was going to give my father's plant to the Black Panthers. I wanted the business to be run on an anti-capitalist system of profit sharing.

The second night of the riots I had stayed up most of the night listening to the radio following the events.

There was firebombing all over the black neighborhoods and a dusk to dawn curfew. My father broke curfew and left for the plant, which was about two miles away. I was in my room listening to the radio when they called for volunteers to meet who wanted to help stop the rioting. It was a call to meet at first light at a specific address in the ghetto. I snuck out of the house and went to volunteer.

At the meeting place we were given metal helmets. We were loaded into the back of an open truck. The helmets were provided to protect our heads from sniper fire. It was the first time I was shot at. The truck took us to a bombed out drug store. We were given brooms and we swept up all the broken glass.

The owner was there who lived in my neighborhood and he recognized me. He was a survivor of the concentration camps from WWII. He was publically a liberal and supported civil rights even though his store was bombed. Several months later he was shot to death during a robbery in his pharmacy. My parents since have reflected and said it was a difficult time to raise kids.

My friends and I hated the establishment and supported all the ideas of what was called the New Left.

We wore our uniform of bell-bottoms and beads and long hair and sandals, and conformed to the New Left Party line. I also went to SDS meetings. SDS stood for Students for a Democratic Society. They developed and expanded rapidly in the mid-1960s as a student group that represented the alternative to the Republicans and Democrats or so called establishment.

The New Left was anti-war and anti-imperialist. Before their demise, they were responsible for students getting increased power at universities and campuses around the country.

The American New Left was different for me than the New Left in Europe. Many of the American leaders here were Jewish, such as Abbie Hoffman, Jerry Rubin and were against the war in Vietnam. I do not think they had hatred towards Israel the way the left did in Europe.

I supported a two state solution and Resolution 242 from the United Nations and the return to the 1967 borders with modifications. I did not support the extremist views of the P.L.O.

Trenton was an area that was poor and to say the least rough around the edges. People like that tended to hang out in ethnic gangs. Jews lived in one area, Blacks in another. Polish had their own neighborhood. So I was labeled a Jew and that stuck with me. That's why I was so influenced by what was going on in Israel. If the Jewish homeland was having a bad day I would have a bad day. So my upbringing established a pattern of me identifying with the state of Israel.

I studied and read about a political group called The Weathermen. They were a more militant offshoot from Students for a Democratic Society. They were composed mainly from the national leadership of Students for a Democratic Society. Their platform was against the war in Vietnam and they were in support of the civil rights movement of the late 1960s. With revolutionary positions characterized by Black Liberation rhetoric, the group conducted a campaign of bombings through the 1960s and 1970s, including aiding the jailbreak of Timothy Leary.

After the riots cooled it was all about peace marches to protest the war in Vietnam. We were all facing the draft upon finishing high school. I had decided to go to Canada rather than fight. I went to demonstrations in NYC and Philadelphia.

It was a great place to meet women. At these counter culture events free love was the order of the day. That's why many of my friends went. They were a lot of fun and usually rock bands would play at these events. In public I would date women with average body types, but in private I was obsessing about my sexual desire with Rubenesque women. I enjoyed zaftig women because there was more to love. We also went to these events called be-ins. They took place in Central Park in New York City. People smoked weed, tripped, engaged in protest and made love.

By the time I got my driver's license I had started to grow my hair long. There was a lot of division in society then. It was class warfare and the Conservatives hated the Hippies and the New Left.

I remember one day I went for a ride in my new second hand car I got when I was seventeen. It was a Volkswagen bug and it had psychedelic flowers painted all over it. In the morning I got pulled over and given two tickets. One was for driving bare foot and the other was for making a wrong turn.

The police loved pulling over hippies or guys with long hair. Later that afternoon I went for a drive and got pulled over again and was given more tickets. It was like every time I left the house I was pulled over for having long hair.

Billy Selesnick

In Trenton High the teachers told us that if we were suspected of having the potential of being subversive they were supposed to report it. That meant to the government. Then they would have a file on you. Some teachers did and others did not support it.

The New Jersey state troopers had the worst reputation for harassing hippies. They pulled over some suspected Black Panthers on the New Jersey turnpike and that incident lead to some murders and one of the Panthers getting asylum in Cuba. Once, when I was on West State Street in front of the New Jersey State House, a state trooper told me to pull over. He brought me in to the State House, handcuffed me to a chair, and called my father. I had a bad relationship with my father. He was verbally abusive about my politics, my appearance, my schoolwork. I had a better relationship with my mother who was more understanding. Finally, he let me go with a handful of tickets. My father was embarrassed about every aspect of my being. I knew he did not like me. He would say why don't you go play in the traffic.

My friends and I smoked grass and hash. We hung around a luncheonette where a lot of long hairs went. We were constantly under surveillance and had our phones tapped. There were a lot of undercover agents who masqueraded as long hair New Lefties. Some were committed pacifists but were busted and turned agents to stay out of jail.

Sex, Drugs and Rock and Roll were the order of the day . . . at least in our crowd. Thinking back, we all hoped for liberty, equal rights and to the end of wars.

My sister's emotional problems had gotten worse. My father had my sister arrested for not coming home at night and staying at her boyfriend's house. He was a few years older than her. She then ran away with a girlfriend and it took my parents a month to find her.

She was just twelve years old. I could not wait until I was eighteen so I could legally move out of my house. On the day I did move out something happened that I have a lot of guilt about. When I was living at home I was the buffer between my sister and my parents. I always covered for her with my parents. I felt I was the one who was holding the family together. Anyway, when I moved out and went to Woodstock, Mindy ran away again.

She was arrested and put in a prison for girls. She was declared incorrigible and after two weeks went into a lockdown hospital for disturbed children. She remained there for several months. I would come down and visit and go to therapy there. When she was released she resumed a normal life. She went on to raise four wonderful children.

My next acid trip was done on a weekend that my parents were out of town. I was going to trip with my new girlfriend named Cindy. We took our acid around ten in the morning.

By eleven we were in my parents' bed making love. With each thrust, patterns of vibrant colors ran through my head.

Cindy was experiencing the same thing. Conversation again became useless as we were both seeing the same thing and thinking the same thoughts. Every second new images would appear and then dissolve into another. I began climaxing and each drop of semen became giant waves pounding on a beach. Images dissolved from one into another. My climax went on for several hours as we lay intertwined. Each kiss took us further out in a world of colorful psychedelic images. God appeared over our bed as an old man with a long beard. Hundreds of angels stood in back of him blowing trumpets announcing the beginning of a new world.

Billy Selesnick

I heard about Woodstock from a nursing student I sat with on my way to a protest in Philadelphia. She told me about this town near the Catskills in New York State called Woodstock. She said there were a lot of artists and musicians there. It was established in 1770. It played host to numerous Hudson River School painters in the late 1880's

The arts and crafts movement came in 1902 with the arrival of Ralph Whitehead and Hervey White. Whitehead moved there to start a utopian community based on the ideas of Morris, a utopian thinker from England.

From 1915 to 1931, Harvey White started the Maverick art colony that held the Maverick festivals in which hundreds of free spirits, artists, musicians, and writers came for summer long festivals of parties and orgies. It was also considered a sacred place of the American Indians who were the areas first inhabitants.

This woman told me there were many communes there. She said it was nestled in the mountains and the people rode up the mountain and stopped and smoked pot along the way.

It sounded like my kind of place.

There were also a lot of artists there who built way out houses. Some were geodesic domes, others were tree houses and one was built into the side of a cliff and everything in it was wrapped in tin foil.

My time finishing up my high school years was dismal. I was supposed to graduate in 1969

1969 but did not have enough credits having failed all my courses. Basically, when my school mates graduated I dropped out, and a month later took my high school equivalency exam and passed. If you did not go directly to college, you would be drafted into the army in a matter of months. I knew at this point I wanted to go into the arts. I had begun to experiment with sculpture, drawing and watercolor.

Chapter Two

So, in May 1969 my friend and I took the bus up to Woodstock, New York in the Catskills. We knew Bob Dylan lived there and a host of other well-known musicians. It was a charming mountain village with cafes and art galleries. We found a room to rent and both got jobs washing dishes at the Purple Elephant, a restaurant and music club. It was an old barn that was on Rock City Road, a block from the village green.

I was going to apply for conscientious objector status so I did not have to go in the army. Since I moved to Woodstock, I changed my draft board from Trenton, New Jersey, to Kingston, New York. There was a group located in Woodstock who counseled people who were against the war. They told you what to say when you were interviewed by the draft board.

Within two weeks at the Purple Elephant I was head cook. One of the cooks quit and I asked for his job. They gave me the position because I was good in the kitchen. I had been on a macrobiotic diet. I had started that in New Jersey while in high school. They had macrobiotic dishes on the menu. One of the reasons I got the job was that I knew how to cook vegetarian food.

That summer Jimmy Hendrix came into the Purple Elephant ... so did Janis Joplin, Tina Turner, Van Morrison and Paul Butterfield. I thought I had died and gone to heaven. I was able to rub shoulders with the stars of our day.

All was not perfect in town. There was a sort of war going on at that time between the hippies and the more conservative members of the community. The police and the state police known as B.C.I. sided with the more conservative members of the community.

I was arrested on the village green for not wearing a shirt. It was summer and it was ninety degrees and a bunch of like minded people were sitting on the benches in the center of town. Next thing you know a police car pulls up and arrests all of us. We were let go in a few hours. We had to pay a small fine.

A lot of the communes got raided and hippies were beat up and arrested. This went on for a few years. There were horrible fights at town hall meetings on Friday nights. The farmers and rednecks mostly hated the hippies. There was an element of the older more conservative artists that did not like flower children. Some of them had emigrated from Europe and had right wing views.

The flower children had started moving to Woodstock in the mid 1960's when Bob Dylan and other well-known folk singers moved there. There were already a lot of artists living there, but this new influx was hippies and a lot of communes began sprouting up.

The hippies who were all about love thought Woodstock was a type of utopian community. It definitely was a town full of free spirits. All the free sprits competed with each other as to who could be the most outrageous.

Woodstock was also famous for a festival in 1969. It was called the Woodstock Music and Art Fair. It was called A Aquarian Exposition of Three Days of Peace and Music. It was held at Max Yeager's six-hundred-acre dairy farm in the Catskills, next to the hamlet of Whitelake in the town of Bethel, New York, from August fifteenth to August eighteenth in It was in Sullivan County, which is forty-three miles from the town of Woodstock During the sometimes rainy weekend, thirty-two acts performed outdoors in front of five hundred thousand concert goers. It was widely regarded as a pivotal moment in the history of rock and roll. Rolling Stone listed it as one of the fifty moments that changed the history of rock and roll. The event was captured in the 1970 movie documentary called *Woodstock*. An accompanied sound track album with Joni

Mitchell's song "Woodstock," commemorated the event and became a major hit for Crosby, Stills, Nash and Young.

Woodstock is famous for the festival that took place in Bethel in August. It used the Woodstock name because Michael Lang, the producer, lived in Woodstock and Bethel was the closest place he could find. So, in the middle of August a few of us at the Purple Elephant Restaurant left a day early for the festival. It was already crowded when we got there. We camped out at what was known as the hog farm. That was the name of a commune in New Mexico. They were at the site running the free kitchen. We even had a private stage there.

There are no words to describe the social and political implications of this weekend of music and art ... the music, the energy and the connection with all the people who felt the same way. We were against the war and we wanted freedom. It was unbelievable because it made you believe that dreams can come true and peace is possible. It was an amazing moment in history for me and thousands of others around the world. In retrospect, I feel it shortened the war in Vietnam and helped bring about the end of the Iron Curtain. It was a blue jean rock and roll revolution ... my hero Abbie Hoffman was there, on acid, getting in a fight on stage with one of the members of the band, The Who.

After the concert I went back to Woodstock and

found out that they were mad at me because I went to the festival without finding a replacement for my shifts cooking. I no longer had a job there.

I was planning to begin art studies in the fall. I had been accepted to Art Career School on top of the Flat Iron Building in NYC. It was located at Twenty-Third Street and Fifth Ave. The Flat Iron Building was an historical monument because it was the first skyscraper in New York City. It was a commercial as well as fine art school that basically took anybody.

I was commuting from Trenton, returning there shortly after the festival. My father was just glad I was in school. He worked eighteen hours a day anyway. He was often away. We did not like each other. We tolerated each other. He was for Nixon then and still did not like artists, hippies, gays, or communists.

I had a girlfriend by then. I saw her at nights or weekends. Her name was Cindy I was attracted to her because I saw her as a rebel or bad girl. She had already gotten in trouble for drugs. She was different and did not tow the line. She also liked art. She dressed really cool. We called ourselves freaks.

Cindy was medium height and slender built with brown hair, wild hippy style. She had small breasts. Most guys liked big breasted women. I still had my secret fantasy of buxom girls.

She lived in Lawrenceville in-between Trenton and Princeton. I met her when my best friend took her on a date where we doubled. We went to a rock and roll show in Philadelphia. We were going to see the Grateful Dead at the Electric Factory we went in my jeep Willy. We were smoking weed along the way.

Billy Selesnick

ONE OF MY EARLY PAINTINGS

I towed the left wing party line. I had long hair and a pierced ear. There was a percentage of the population who thought like me. The ones that didn't usually were either hostile or curious. I smoked weed and knew a lot of drug dealers

Basically, if you smoked you had to have a dealer. So that's how you got to know black market drug dealers. Everybody that smoked usually ended up dealing to one extent or the other.

Some of my friends went on to make literally millions. One who did got shot. He saved a million in cash by dealing. He had done some time in a reform school, and then he did a little time near the Belle Mountain ski area. It was behind a quarry. It was called the Mercer County Workhouse. I painted the quarry in front of it all the time. He then planned to move to

Paris with his prostitute girlfriend. She set him up with some French gangster, who shot and killed him. She got half the cash and came back to the states.

Others were busted and went bankrupt. Many just dealt enough to support their habit. I never was into hard drugs. I knew people who used the needle, but I didn't. I always looked up to the big dealers and players. I would run errands. Plus, you did what you did to get free weed or acid.

That May, when my semester ended at art school, my girlfriend Cindy and I moved back to the hamlet of Woodstock. I was going to take courses at the Arts Student League Summer School which was located there. Cindy would pose for me when I was learning to do nudes. We got along well and liked the same things. We would walk to the Millstream Motel and swim in the stream there.

That was the summer of 1970. There were over twenty galleries in town then. Woodstock was in its heyday. There were communes, ashrams yoga centers, health food stores, monasteries, all kinds of alternative lifestyle courses and schools. There were music clubs with top international acts.

There was a macrobiotic restaurant run by volunteers. First I waited tables at the Espresso Café, owned then by Bernard Pateral, who was Bob Dylan's body guard and chef. He was from Paris and was an expert knife thrower. Dylan wrote one of his most famous albums there.

Then I worked for Rom Merian, who opened the Joyous Lake. I washed dishes there, and saw many great acts up close. I got to be on a first name basis and personal friends with Charlie Mingus who played there. Cindy and I were also invited to Keith Richards's birthday party there. The Rolling stones were in town then recording Steel Wheels. Mick Jagger was there.

You would walk through the center of town and think it was Halloween. People dressed in wild tie-dye and long flowing robes. There were sacred mushroom drum circles that lasted all night long. Everybody would be tripping on mushrooms. There was a Tibetan monastery on top of Meade Mountain that was handpicked by the Dalai Lama.

Actually there is this sacred place called Meade Meadow just over the other side of the mountain. It was just past Father Francis Church and the Tibetan monastery.

That's where Cindy and I were married in 1971. Meade Meadow was a place in the late 1960s and early 1970s where a lot of alien encounters took place there. A renegade Episcopal minister of a church in the center of town married us. His name was Abel. When he first arrived in town he was very clean cut and conservative. After living in Woodstock for a short while he began to change. His hair became longer. He grew a beard. He wore sandals. He began to have affairs. He dropped acid. At his Sunday services, hippies started attending, to the dismay of his flock. He suddenly began preaching about the benefits of a hippy life style. He became anti government and a radical pacifist. He espoused marijuana and LSD. His flock tried to have him fired but to no avail. He had an iron clad contract. Abel and I would have long discussions about the history of the Jewish holy books.

The Christians called it the Old Testament. The Hebrews called it the Torah. In Jewish circles the origin of the Torah was in dispute. Orthodox and Conservatives believed the Holy Books were written by God himself and the origins were not opened for discussions. The reform movement which was the most liberal had other views. They believed as historians and academics, that the Jewish books could be attributed to certain writers. That different books came from different periods in ancient history. They developed in academic circles of Biblical scholarship which is known as the J.E.P.D. sources. The D period stood for the Book of Deuteronomy. The E period stood for the Exodus period. Accordingly, the style of the prose of each book determined the different time period. Some writers were also identified as women scribes and philosophers.

I was most intrigued by what was called psychedelic art- wild colorful paintings of drug induced hallucinations. I liked the surrealists, symbolists and magic realism. I was mostly doing figure studies of male and female nudes. I tried to develop a more drug induced surrealistic style but lacked the experience and technique. I also posed for a lot of very famous artists. I posed for portraits and in the nude for groups.

The Arts Students League was a famous Art School in New York City. It had a summer school in Woodstock. It was in operation then so I took classes with Robert Angelock and Bruce Dorfman, both highly regarded painters. I concentrated on anatomy, perspective, still life and landscapes.

Meade Mountain had a Zen monastery on the top. This was a quarter of a mile before you got to Meade Meadow. It was located at the site of an old hotel. The Dali Lama picked it out himself. Right before the Zen monastery was Father Francis' hand built Catholic Church. He was a renegade priest. He was excommunicated from the church for marrying blacks and whites in the 1920's. He came to Woodstock to tutor Ralph Whitehead's children. Whitehead was one of the founding fathers of the art community. Father Francis also had a large flock of parishioners. Many were conservative. Hippies started attending his church. He became a revered figure in the underground movement in the Woodstock area. He was always getting in trouble with his conservative flock for being unconventional. His hand built church was made using trees whole like a log cabin. The trees were never made into planks and the bark was left on them. He lived in a small one room cabin next to his church.

He had taken his vows of poverty as a young priest and kept them.

The Arts Student League Summer School was also bringing in respected guest speakers. That is where I met Isaac Abrams, a psychedelic painter. He was the one who turned me on to a painter from Vienna Austria named Ernst Fuchs. He and his friends painted in a style called The Vienna School of Fantastic Realism. It was the Old Masters' technique and style combined with fantasy. It reminded me of Hieronymus Bosch and Salvador Dali. I was very influenced and inspired by Fuchs and the Vienna School of Fantastic Realism.

That fall Cindy and I decided to stay in Woodstock. I was going to study with a well-known older artist who mostly painted nudes and landscape. His name was Frank Brockenshaw but was known as Brock.

I got a part time job cooking in another restaurant. Cindy got a job waitressing. She also modeled regularly for Brock. I painted and worked for the next year. We enjoyed all the concerts and events Woodstock had to offer that year.

Cindy also got pregnant. During these years I think Cindy and I got along pretty well. We had the same interests and coexisted well together. Neither of us was flirtatious with members of the opposite sex so there was little conflict.

So we loaded up our Volkswagen bus and decided

to move to Santé Fe, New Mexico. We got the idea and information from reading the Whole Earth Catalog which was basically an encyclopedia of alternative living. It listed many communes that were around the country.

It also taught you how to live outside the system without using money.

Our first night arriving in town there was a cultural festival taking place in the center of town. Santé Fe was home to three ethnic groups: The American Indians, the White man known as Anglos, short for Anglo-Saxon, and the Chicanos who were Spanish. Then in the 1960s hippies started arriving, adding to the volatile mix. Relationships between these groups were tense. There were some problems between the Chicanos and the police. As we drove into the center of town, we witnessed rioting between Spanish teenagers and the police. Cindy and I witnessed teenagers armed with home-made Molotov cocktails engaged in street battles with the police.

In the mid 1960's there was a hippy commune outside of town that was attacked by conservative redneck Anglos who were aligned with the Anglo ranch owners. There was armed conflict and a rape. Then there was retaliation by the hippies and some murders took place. The movie Billy Jack, which was released in 1972, was based on those incidents.

We heard there were a lot of artists there. We read there were different communes and people who lived in geodesic domes. We knew the Hog Farm Commune was in Taos.

We found an apartment on Canyon Road. We both got part time jobs and I painted at home in my free time. Cindy had not yet begun to show and could still work. We also started a candle-making business. We would make them in our apartment in Santa Fe and take them on weekends to a flea market sixty miles away in Albuquerque. Along the way there was a turnoff, which took you on a dirt road to a town called Cuba, New Mexico. That was in Indian Territory. In Cuba there were hot springs. Around the turn of the century an adobe one story resort was built around this spring. The water was piped into a swimming pool and a courtyard was built around it. The water was at a constant one hundred and ten degrees. A few years previously some hippies leased this resort from the owners and started a commune. The flower children greatly admired the traditions of the American Indian and adopted it in their use of Peyote as a religious sacrament, their harmony with nature and living off the land, their native dress, their long hair, and their communion with nature and spirits.

Some Indians would come to the springs to relax and party. There were some unpleasant incidents between the hippies and the Indians. The flower children had the reputation of espousing free love. This led to some aggressive behavior between the Indians and the women at the hot springs. There were several rapes. The hippies started arming themselves with rifles, and relationships between the Indians and the hippy women became very tense. As with all people there were several different types of Indians. The rapes occurred with some alcoholic Indians who had crew cuts. They had rejected some of the values of the more traditional Indians and taken on the values of redneck white men. The Indians who had long hair did better with the white women at the commune.

Cindy and I discovered these hot springs when we would go to Albuquerque to sell our candles. We had many wonderful experiences there. We also went to hot springs in the mountains near Taos. Taos was more of an artist center than Santa Fe. Georgia O'Keefe, a famous female artist who became well known for her erotic depiction of flowers, lived there in the 1920's.

We spent a year there, and Cindy gave birth to our son, who we named Joshua. After a year in Santa Fe, we moved back to Woodstock. We found a cottage in the center of town and I shared a little garage studio with a friend. I waited tables and focused on my art. I had already sold some of my paintings for modest prices. I found that my more traditional works sold better than the far-out surreal paintings I did. I loved the Surrealists. They often worked from their dreams. I had this dream. I was twelve years old, and I was learning Torah. I left the service and went to the basement of the temple. I discovered some secret steps. They went down to a secret room of prayer. Inside were the holy men. A service within a service within a service. I stood unobserved and watched the secret rites of the inner sanctum. I finally was able to paint that dream.

At this time in Woodstock I was turned on to this group of painters called the Vienna School of Fantastic Realism. They were mostly from Vienna, Austria. Their paintings were exactly like the name, fantastic realism. It was led by a man named Ernst Fuchs. He had a long biblical beard and hair that went to the middle of his back. He kept that hidden under a Turkish Fez. He had the eyes of a biblical prophet. He had a Rasputin like beard and a Svengali like effect on people. His paintings were technically superb with a style like the old masters. His etchings rivaled the famous German artist Albrecht Durer. His subject matter was what I would describe as biblical apocalyptic. Many of his paintings were surrealistic. Fuchs, a Jew, was recognized as a child prodigy. His work commanded very high prices. He led an extravagant life style living in castles throughout Europe. His only rival at that time was Salvador Dali. I liked Dali's work a lot. However, I identified more with Fuchs because of his Jewish and Old Testament themes. He was having a show at that time. It was at the Auberbach Gallery on Madison Ave. in New York City. I took the bus from Woodstock to see the show.

The name of Fuch's movement was the Vienna School of Fantastic Realism. There were other artists living in Vienna, Austria that were painting in that style. One was named Eric Braurer. He painted in a colorful dream like style that was very surrealistic and "other worldly." Another artist in that group was named Rudolf Hausner. He was German and painted these surreal nightmares like images of his wartime experiences in the German navy. Another artist that studied with that group was named H.R. Giger. He was Swiss and after working with Fuchs went on to create the special effects for the "Alien" movies starring Sigourney Weaver. I really liked this style and group of artists. I wanted to be able to paint like them. There was a group of artists in Woodstock who felt the way I did and they were emulating their strange style. This one artist who lived in Woodstock named Isaac Abrams who was a famous psychedelic artist had gone to Europe to study with Fuchs in a castle in Spain. It was rumored that Dali was there. Isaac's work was mostly hallucinations from his acid trips. Timothy Leary collected his work. When Isaac got back from Europe he told the artist community in Woodstock that Fuchs was doing a seminar in a castle outside of Vienna. Visionary artists from all over the world were going to be there. It was to be held at the Castle Warholz near Vienna in the woods. I decided that I wanted to go. I had never been to Europe. I decided to leave my wife and son in Woodstock and do the trip alone. The seminar was in the summer of 1972.

I booked my ticket on Icelandic Airways. After a stop- over in Iceland we landed in Brussels and I was going to take the train to Vienna. Instead, I did a detour to Amsterdam on the way. I experienced the hash bars and the hippy scene at Vondel Park. Finally, after a few days in Amsterdam, I decided to see Paris the art capitol of the world. Paris did not disappoint me and I decided one day I was going to bring my family to Paris to live while I studied art. From Paris I made my way to the castle in the woods outside of Vienna.

The castle was located in what was a small farming community. It was a country town that had lovely B and B's on its tree lined streets. The castle was walking distance away. At one time it belonged to the Kaiser Wilhelm. It was rented by Fuchs for the summer. On the first day after arriving Fuchs was scheduled to make an appearance. He was a demi God to the other artists. Fuchs sold his work to international celebrities from all over the world. There was a competition between Dali and Fuchs on who got more money for their work. Both were world famous and had large out of control egos. Fuchs made his appearance with his beautiful much younger wife. He had been married numerous times and had a large brood of children, many were with him when he made his grand entrance to the castle. He was wearing very expensive silk pants. He had what looked like a nice European hand-made smoking jacket on and his trademark fez covering his long hair which was tied and put under his hat. His long Rasputin like beard was tucked into the top of shirt. He looked like some eccentric millionaire pasha. He talked to each student individually giving his critiques. When my turn came he complimented a self- portrait I showed him and suggested an idea for a painting he wanted me to start tomorrow.

All the artists were staying at the charming B and B. There were communal dinners at night where we would talk about art. I stayed a few weeks making friends and creating art. These artists were not just realists; they were inspired visionaries. At the end of my trip I was going to take the train from Vienna to the South of France to visit my parents who were living there. I changed trains in Venice, Italy and took a stroll around the train station and along the canals. My parents were living in Mandelieu, a few miles from Cannes. I visited with them for a few days before I returned to the states.

When I returned to Woodstock I was really gung ho on this fantastic realism style. I still found that I needed more classical techniques in order to express myself. I painted as much as I could.

I also had a part time job on a garbage truck. Half the things we found we could sell or recycle. The garbage truck job was the best part time job I ever had in my life. We would find all kinds of valuable garbage and then pass it on to the "free store" in town. That was a store where everything was free. We also collected the garbage at the local supermarket. They would always throw away cans that were damaged. We would collect them and either resell them or give them away. I became very popular when I had that job.

There were always women waiting for us when we would go to their house to collect garbage. There was this one pleasingly plump woman who would wait in the garage for me. Cindy at first didn't knew about my secret life and obsession with big women. When she began to have her suspicions she was not really threatened by it. She knew I was always seeking out Rubenesque women to paint and she was amused by it. I got the garbage at all the local celebrities' houses. I picked up trash at Bob Dylan's house, Paul

Butterfield's, and from members of the Band who lived at a house called Big Pink. A famous album was made there.

Cindy and I continued to get along well and rarely fought. I loved taking care of our son and was willing and eager to take on those responsibilities.

My boss's wife went to school at a place called Goddard College in Plainfield, Vermont. Goddard was a private liberal arts college. It offered undergraduate and graduate programs. It had an independent study program where you could do the work at home. You would go up there two weeks every six months to meet with students in your cycle and your professors.

This sounded perfect. I decided to enroll. I had some advanced standing because I went to art school in New York City for a year. Also I had had private studies with Brock and Fuchs. That counted for something. Goddard had the reputation of being ahead of its time. Many of the professors were well known leftists.

For example, one professor was a member of the Black Panther party.

His name was George Ware, and was also one of the founders of SNCC. That stood for Student Non-violent Coordination Committee, which was one of the organizations of the American Civil Rights Movement in the 1960s. It emerged from a series of student meetings led by Ellis Baker at Shaw University in April 1960. SNCC leaders included H. Rap Brown and Stokley Carmichael. In the 1960's he also met Che Guevara at a meeting. George Ware later joined the Black Panther Party. He was one of my first teachers at Goddard and I liked and respected him very much.

Another professor was one of the guys who were part of the Chicago Seven. There were seven defendants: Abbie Hoffman, Jerry Rubin, Tom

Hayden, Rennie Davis, John Froines, Lee Weiner, and David Dellinger. They were charged with conspiracy to riot at the Chicago 1968 Democratic National Convention. David Dellinger was a radical pacifist and the author of many books. He died May 25th in Montpelier, Vermont, home to Goddard College.

At Goddard, one had to write his own study plan and have it approved by his mentor or professor after which, there would be continuous correspondence. With this program you could get college credit for work done at home. Once enrolled, I went up to Goddard to write my study plan, which was to paint and draw, and study the Old Testament. (I loved those stories and wanted to do paintings of them). Then I went back to Woodstock to complete my goals. I would return to Goddard in Plainfield, Vermont six months later to present my project. When we returned to present our projects is when the fun began. Many of the students were married or had significant others at home. Now we were away from them and many of the students had affairs. Goddard had a reputation for sex, drugs and rock and roll. It was then that our marriage began to show some cracks. Every time I went up there for a cycle change, I had a different girlfriend.

I read about Che Guevarra, Fidel Castro, Marx, Lenin, Ho Chi Minh, Herman Hesse, and Carl Jung. I even read every book translated into English by Solzhenitsyn. When Patty Hearst was kidnapped, I was on the side of the Symbionese Liberation Army. Luckily, a few others in Woodstock and Goddard were too. It did not mean that we would plant a bomb against the establishment. It meant that a small but significant percentage of the population was sympathetic to groups like the Black Panthers or other radical groups. Vietnam and civil right were the main issues that caused radicalization of many of my friends.

We believed in a benevolent socialism. A government which had no restrictions in our freedoms. Many young people had posters of Che Guevarra in their rooms. That was the mentality of the day. A good friend of mine went on a secret trip to Cuba through Mexico to cut sugar cane. My friend came back with stories of how Fidel himself would show up and work out in the fields with all the young people. Living a life style between Goddard and Woodstock worked for me at the time. It was nice being surrounded by like-minded people.

After completing my first cycle at Goddard, I got more ambitious and applied for their European Master's program. My course was to go and study for my Master's degree in Paris, France.

My relationship with Cindy had grown more unstable since my involvement with Goddard. We had several big fights and almost broke up because of affairs we both had when I was away at Goddard. However, she liked the idea of moving to France, so we decided to give our relationship another chance.

The head of the European Master's program was named Doctor Tony Pierce, and he accepted me as one of his students. We were to meet every six months with the other students that were working in Europe. Our first meeting was in Devon, England, at a place called Dartington Hall in Totnes, England. Dartington Hall was a famous art school.

It was also a medieval castle with jousting grounds. It was built between 1388 and 1400 for John Holand Earl of Huntington. I never saw anything like it. The houses in the area had thatched roofs.

I was getting student loans. I was working part time and saving money. Cindy worked and made a contribution. My parents helped a little and gave a couple hundred a month. Also, I had a modest success with selling my paintings to friends and some drug dealers.

My study plan was to copy the Old Masters paintings to improve my drawing and painting technique and to make drawings of biblical period artifacts and sculpture in the Louvre.

In 1674 King Louis XIV of France moved the seat of royal power from the Louvre to Versailles and the Louvre was converted into a meeting place for artistic and intellectual salons. The Louvre had eight miles of hallways on three floors.

The Louvre had a department Oriental. That was where I would do my biblical paintings. I would be familiar with how things looked in those days. Little did I know that many spies went undercover and hung out in the near eastern department of the Louvre.

This program allowed you to have what's called core faculty who was Dr. Tony Pierce at Goddard. Then there was field faculty. That was if you found an expert in your field and they agree to tutor you. Then they would be eligible to get a financial stipend from Goddard.

There was another female student working with Goddard at the time. She was studying art history and had a teacher that worked as a tour guide at the Louvre. A tour guide at the Louvre had to have a PHD. Her name was Madame Augarde. She agreed to work with me at the Louvre.

The hippy scene – or then what was called the underground in Europe, I found out – was more political and violent than in the states. There were the Red Brigades in Italy and Baeder Meinhof in Germany. In France you had many radical student groups and militants.

The Iron Curtain had not yet fallen. In France, the Communist Party was legal and was a legitimate political party. In the states it was much different. There were some bombing and violence, but it seemed more extreme in Europe.

Also, the flow of ideas was much freer in the states. In Europe then, some books were banned. The Beatles were banned from playing in Israel.

The United States was and is the best place to be an artist. The communist or socialist party had very little support in the states.

We said goodbye to our friends in Woodstock. Now I was Goddard's representative in Paris. I said goodbye to a friend with whom I worked and who owned a garbage truck company. His wife was the one that turned me on to Goddard. Then we left Woodstock and drove directly to J.F.K. We left our dog Micah with some friends. We said goodbye to Woodstock, the counter culture, and we said goodbye to the United States of America.

Chapter Three

In 1972 at the Munich Olympics, eleven Israeli athletes were murdered by the Black September Palestinian terrorists. According to legend and George Jonas' book, Israeli Prime Minister Golda Meir put together a squad of men to revenge this terrible act. Israel to this day denies this squad exists. The men in the PLO that committed this heinous deed were going to be murdered. It was an "unofficial un-sanctioned operation."

The Mossad is Israel's intelligence agency. The members of the Mossad who were chosen for this operation resigned from the Mossad upon the start of this mission. It was unofficial, because crimes were going to be perpetrated on foreign soil. If bystanders were killed, Israel could not be seen publicly as sponsoring this act of revenge in other countries.

It was led by a young man in the Mossad whose name was Avner. Avner was given the necessary funds in cash, and his mandate was to kill those responsible for murdering the Israelis at the Munich Olympics.

The assassination of these PLO agents took place in Rome, Paris, Nicosia, Cyprus, Beirut, Lebanon, Athens, Greece, Glarus, Switzerland, and Tarifa, Spain. Avner had safe houses in many of these places. Some innocent people had been killed. To find these Palestinians, large amounts of money had been spent to buy information as to find their location.

In those days' members of the New Left and hippies, especially, in Europe, had ties and sympathies to the Palestinian cause. Avner and his group infiltrated various hippy groups and antiwar organizations and the European Underground as a way to find the guilty Palestinians.

By the time the operation had begun to wind down, several members of Avner's team had been murdered. There was the murder of a prostitute in Holland who was the last person to be with one of the team members who had been killed.

My part of it happened completely by accident and by being in the wrong place at the wrong time.

In 1974 we flew air France from JFK to Paris. We had shipped our things in advance. Our trunks were mostly filled with books on art and art history. The history of Paris spans over ten thousand years. During that time the city grew from a small Gallic settlement into a capitol and primary city of France. It further developed into a center of art, medicine, science, fashion, tourism, high culture and finance. Paris is one of the world's global cities.

My father was working in Europe at the time. My mother and he resided in the south of France. It was a little town called Mandelieu, just behind Lanapoule, which was on the coast near Cannes. My father's business partner came to pick us up. He came with his new young French girlfriend. They were an hour late. We were grateful for the ride and use of an apartment.

My father had an office in Paris in the suburbs in an area called Montrouge, which translated into English is "red mountain." My father was still in the dry cleaning business. He specialized in cleaning leather and suede garments. At that time, he began selling the chemicals he patented especially to clean leather and suede. He was selling them internationally. For some thirty years my father traveled around the world selling his patented chemicals.

There are a number of colorful traditions of the name Montrouge. It appears that the earth has a reddish color in that area. Montrouge was a working class suburb. It was just over the other side of the circular highway that surrounds Paris called peri preriqueou. Montrouge is a commune in the southern Parisian suburbs. It is one of the most densely populated municipalities in Europe.

We had use of a small apartment there while we looked around for a place to live. It was a nice small one-bedroom apartment in a concrete communist style building. My wife and I went to a real estate agency that specialized in finding apartments. Within a week we found a place in the center of Paris in the first arrondissement. It was on Rue de la Jussiene right around the corner from the Grande Post, Paris's main post office. It was a one room studio. It had a small bathroom and kitchen. We got a folding screen and set it up around my son's bed so we all had privacy.

That one room also became my art studio. I would mostly do drawings on a mattress which was on the floor, that was our bed. It was over in the corner in front of a window. Our street was only about one thousand feet long. On one side of the street there was a public school that took up the whole block. On our side of the street there were about fifteen buildings.

There was a balcony in front of each window. On one corner was a typical French bar and café. Across the street was a newspaper stand where I got the International Herald Tribune every day.

It was also very close to what was left of Les Halle, which is located in the first arrondissement, just south of Rue Montorgueil.

Les Halle was a large central wholesale market place which was demolished in 1971. It was now a huge hole a few acres big. The big outdoor produce market which provided food for the restaurants in Paris, had been moved to the suburbs. It was replaced with an underground modern shopping neighbor-hood and metro spot. Les Halle was next to a church called Sainte Eustace.

Memoirs of an Artist

The Church of Saint Eustauce is a church that was built between 1532 and 1632. It is considered a masterpiece of late Gothic architecture. The Church's reputation was considered strong enough to be chosen as the location of a young King Louis the XIV to receive communion. Mozart also chose the location for his mother's funeral. I did many pencil drawings of this church. I would do them plein air, standing on location dealing with the weather and curious people. It was a way to become known in the neighborhood. I made many friends that way.

The market street, then was Rue Montorgueil. This street was one block away from Rue de la Jussienne. The market street is in the second arrondissement. It is lined with restaurants, cafes, bakeries, fish stores, cheese shops, produce, and flower shops. It's known as a place where Parisians socialize while doing their shopping. Many artists have come to this street to paint. Market day was when all the vendors would display their wares outside. The only way I could describe it was that it was like a big carnival. There would also be entertainment. There would be a man with a monkey doing tricks. There would be an accordion player. There would be bands. Claude Monet did a famous painting of all the colors of rue Montorgueil.

There was a communist party office there, as well as a socialist party office. At the time we were in Paris, bombs had gone off several times in their offices. It was a very working class restaurant supply area.

Au Pied de Couchon was my second home. That was a famous restaurant that was next to Metro Les Halles. I picked up a little French while there but I had a hard time learning languages. Cindy and I were getting along well. She was absorbed into her role as mother and shopper. I was equally taken by my new surroundings.

Nights and weekends we did incredible things together. Saturdays, or on warm evenings, we would take these incredible walks with our son to the Quartier Latin. We would take different routes to the river Seine. We loved and got to know the different bridges which crossed from the right to the left bank. My favorite, which was closed to cars, was a walking bridge where artists would set up and paint. That one was by the Louvre. It was called Pont des Arts. On these bridges there would be vendors set up selling old lithos, old engravings, and second hand books. There would also be artists set up painting the view from the bridge plein air. "Plein air" means painting outside in French. That view would be the River Seine with a series of bridges. My favorite view was closer to the Notre Dame Cathedral.

The Louvre is one of the largest museums in the world and is an important historical monument. It is a central landmark of Paris. It is located on the right bank of the River Seine. It feels like it is a mile long; it's so easy to get lost there because it is so immense.

In 1983 President Mitterrand proposed, as one of his grand projects, a new entrance in the shape of a large glass pyramid. The commission was awarded to a famous architect named I.M. Pei. The Louvre was like the Old Testament. The Louvre was a depository of knowledge like the holy books.

Our studio apartment on Rue de la Jussienne was not too far from the Louvre, and I would walk to it 5 or 6 days a week. I would walk by so many famous buildings from all different time periods. It was really overwhelming.

Memoirs of an Artist

COPY OF AN OLD MASTERS PAINTING DONE IN PENCIL

My study plan outlined a course of study where I went to the Louvre to copy the Old Masters, mostly portraits. In the morning I did Old Master copies. In the afternoon I would work in the department Oriental where I would make drawings of sculpture from the period of the Old Testament. In the mornings the galleries where the copyists worked were crowded with tourists. The department Oriental was not crowded at all.

There were many beautiful women who were copyists in the Louvre. They came from all over the world. I could tell how rich they were by the clothes they wore and the smell of their perfume. Working in the Arts was considered an acceptable profession to the middle and upper class women.

DRAWING OF AN OLD TESTAMENT ARTIFACT

There were also many tour groups that would walk by the copyists and comment on our work as well as the painting we would be copying. Besides the tour groups, there were always thousands of tourists walking by and trying to engage the copyists in conversation. It was hard to concentrate on what you were doing when you worked in a famous place like the Louvre. I was learning how to multi-task. I could complete my assignment and maybe get some phone numbers from attractive women, and perhaps a free lunch. I perfected my dog and pony show in this environment.

The one very strange thing about Paris was there were few big boned women in that city. I loved painting zaftig women, and I spent many hours in the Salon that housed the magnificent paintings by Peter Paul Rubens.

Sir Peter Paul Rubens was a Flemish Baroque painter and a proponent of an extravagant

Baroque style that emphasized movement, color and sensuality. He lived from June 28, 1577, to May 30, 1640. He is well known for his Counter Reformation paintings, portraits, landscapes, history, and paintings of myths and allegorical subjects. In addition, he ran a studio in Antwerp that produced painting popular with nobility and art collectors throughout Europe. Rubens was a classically educated humanist, scholar and diplomat. He was knighted by Phillip the fourth, King of Spain and by Charles the first, King of England.

He was the guy who made it okay to love big women. He was like a demi-God to me. I spent more time studying his substantial women than anything. Most of my work as a copyist every day was in the Rubens room. There was a large group of other copyists who worked at The Louvre every day. For two years I walked by the Mona Lisa, five days a week. It was painted by Italian artist Leonardo da Vinci. The Mona Lisa is a portrait of a woman named Lisa who was the wife of Franceso del Giocondo. This painting has been acclaimed to be the best known, most visited and written about piece of art work in the world. It was painted between 1503 and 1506.

I developed love affairs with the art. I would also talk to the paintings. What was weird was that a painting like the Mona Lisa would answer me back. I also had fantasies about climbing inside a painting. I would stand next to the figures that already were in the painting and integrate myself into the scene. I believed in reincarnation and I felt that in another life I could have painted some of the paintings that I was copying or walking by. When I did my copies and replicated their brushwork it was a way to channel that artist. With channeling, you went into a different altered state then a drum trance. When I channeled at the Louvre, large crowds of people watched me and the other artists who were there. Despite all the activity, you zone out and are oblivious to the surroundings. You are then transported to the period of time your artist is from. In one instance it was my favorite painting in the Louvre, Leonardo's painting entitled Virgin of the Rocks. I felt a very strong attachment to this painting. Leonardo was commissioned to paint it during the period he lived in Milan. That was between 1482 and 1499.So that was the time period and place to where I was transported. It was similar to Star Trek.

Lunch was spent in a crowded dining room. There were two different places I could lunch. One was the tourist gift shop dining area. The others were where the Louvre employees went. That was special. You could get a state subsidized four course meal for five francs. I hung with the hot girls who worked the gift shops and organized the tour guides. They were allowed to line jump because they had a shorter lunch break.

After lunch it was a mile hike to the department Oriental. The walk was like walking through a time machine. The hallways lead from one period of history to another. It was like a dream, especially through the furniture sections. The ceilings and moldings were a blast from the Godlike past. The King's bedroom seemed like the size of a football field. The frescos, the moldings, I felt I was a Greek God lead into the mansions on Mount Olympus. Next, walking through the department of Egyptology, was like walking through ancient history.

My afternoon work of drawing biblical era artifacts was in an area where not too many people ventured. In every two rooms there was a guard.

They put the more aggressive guards in that area because nobody came down there. The one guard in my area was a very loud bipolar alcoholic. After lunch, he would come back drunk, laughing and loudly talking to himself. Once you had a job in Paris you were in a union. It was very hard to lose your job because the union would protect you.

I was spending my afternoons making drawings of a small figurine called Pazuzu. He was from ancient Mesopotamia. It looked like an alien being.

I believed in UFOs. I also believed I saw what looked like an alien one night in a dream- like state. I had awakened and to the side of my bed facing me was a being. It was composed of an illuminated green light.

I opened my eyes and when I saw this creature, I thought I was going to die. I wanted to wake Cindy who was sleeping next to me. I was frozen. I tried to open my mouth and I could not talk. I watched him watching me. We were communicating non-verbally. He said he was an inter-dimensional being from far away.

He told me he was ten thousand years old. He was male and he was very wise. As I looked at him his light would brighten and darken as if he were breathing.

Actually, Pazuzu and I had just gotten back from what I call a magic carpet ride. We saw some things from this magic carpet such as different cities in different parts of the world, from above. Then we returned to my house in the mountains of New York State. Along the way we had a more detailed conversation. I was allowed to ask seven questions. Within the frame work of these questions, all the answers to the origins of the universe were answered.

Billy Selesnick

PAINTING OF PAZUZU, OIL ON BOARD

I was drawing this figurine, which looked like my nighttime experience, when I met a guy named Avner. I did not know it at the time, but he was the leader of the hit squad to avenge the murders at Munich. Golda Meir had picked him to lead the mission. Operation Wrath of God was the name giver to this operation. They were giver a list with eleven names on it. The first man Avner's team found was named Wael Zwaiter. He was a poet and translator.

He was the PLO's representative in Rome. The Mossad had reason to believe that Zwaiter was one of the organizers of terrorism in Europe. He was the translator for *A Thousand and One Nights*.

Also, in 1972, he attempted to blow up an El Al jet by means of a tape recorder bomb carried aboard as a gift by an English women. The captain of this plane had managed to turn back, land safely in Rome, and the two Palestinian hijackers were arrested. Zwaiter was fourth on Golda's list, but he was the first victim of the Israelis. Avner and one of his partners, shot him in the foyer of his apartment building in Rome. I found this out by reading a book by George Jonas called Vengeance. It was the book that inspired Steven Spielberg's movie called Munich.

First on the list of targets was Ali Hassan Salameh, a Palestinian in his thirties, regarded as being the man who was most responsible for the Munich massacre. Despite repeated attempts to get him, Avners' team was not able to find him.

Listed second was Abu Daoud. He was the explosive expert in the Black September Organization. Number Three on the list was Mahmoud Hamshiri, an intellectual and diplomat, and a spokesman for the Palestinian people. Wael Zwaiter, a poet was fourth on the list. Neither he nor Hamshiri were considered to be terrorist leaders. Fifth was Dr. Basil al-Kubasiwas, an arms dealer. In sixth position was Kamal Nasser, public relations chief for Al Fatah and spokesman for the PLO. Kemal Adwan was number seven and in charge of sabotage operations for Al Fatah in Israeli occupied lands. Number eight was Yussef Najjer, one of the highest ranking Palestinian officials who was responsible for the liaison between Al Fatah and Black September.

Mohammed Boudia was number nine. He was an Algerian actor, theater director, well known throughout Paris as a ladies' man rather than an international terrorism figure of significant importance. Number ten was Hussein Abad al-Chir, the PLO's primary contact with the KGB. The last man on the list was Doctor Wadi Haddad who was the mastermind of terrorism. When I met Avner, the only three left on the list were Salameh, Daoud and

Haddad. The others had been killed.

Avner approached me to check out my work. We started a conversation. He spoke English with an Israeli accent. He had very blue eyes, looked very fit, and was a little shorter than me. He looked like a tennis player who went to Yale. He had a very intelligent face, was friendly, warm and very curious.

I told him I went to Goddard College in Vermont and was doing my study plan in Paris. Then I told him that I lived in Woodstock and had gone to the Woodstock Festival. He said, "wow!" and wanted to know all about it.

Then I told him I met Jimi Hendrix personally and he was really impressed. He seemed really interested in communes in the states. He was curious about counter culture. We talked about many things. We talked about Arthur Koestler's book about the Khazers and its implications to the state of Israel. I told him it did not matter if Ashkenazi Jews were Khazer converts. They inherited the souls of being Jewish and suffered the consequences during the Holocaust.

The Khazers were a tribe of people that lived in parts of Turkey. They were nomadic people who were very good with horses, and lived in round houses made of trees. These houses were collapsible due to their nomadic nature. The Khazers were tall and many had red hair and white skin. Geographically, to the west of them the people were Christians, to the east the people were Moslems. They flourished between 800 and 1200 B.C. They were mostly traders and horsemen by profession. They were being pressured to convert to either Christianity or Islam because of their businesses. They chose to convert to Judaism rather than give in to the Christians or Moslems. They were, therefore, not Jews who had a bloodline to King David and the tribes of Israel.

Avner told me he wanted to bring a man back to meet me. He described him as a sort of teacher and he wanted me to tell him that story. The next day he arrived at the designated hour. A very soulful looking old man with deep set eyes was with him. The man was not tall. He looked like he had read many books and had experienced many things. He looked like a philosopher/soldier with the soul of a poet.

I introduced myself and shook his hand. I felt these vibrations that took me to somewhere I had never been, but that was so familiar. It was then I noticed the numbers tattooed on his arm. He did not speak English. Avner began translating while I told my theories on the Khazers and their implication to the state of Israel. The older man said he was not feeling well as they had walked a long way to get there. He said it was from an old leg injury. I had no idea who this man was but I knew he was someone very special and well known. I found out later that he was a former head of the Mossad.

Avner said he was coming back later to talk. When he came back he told me he worked for a successful international company that had offices all over Europe. He traveled back and forth between Rome, Paris, Germany, and he had apartments in each city. I said, "wow, seems like a cool job. Is there anything I could do to help?" I was asking him for a job. He asked me how well I spoke French. I said poorly, but I was learning. He said a second language would help. He said he would think about some things I could do to help out. Then we talked about the Mossad. He said that guys in the Mossad would do more than one thing; you could be in college and be there on a Mossad scholarship and be used when needed.

The subject came up because I sensed that Avner

was really intelligent and the Mossad was intelligence. He seemed to know a lot about it and I just figured he could have been in the Mossad before he was working for this big company. He told me he was in the Israeli army and liked it and did well. Israel was a young country and people wore many hats. I had also heard and read that Israel craved cultural contacts. I think it was all the isolation at the UN.

He then told me that his job required him to sometimes play the role of a journalist. He was doing a story on the Red Brigades in Rome. The Red Brigades were a Marxist Leninist terrorist organization. It was based in Italy. The Red Brigades were responsible for many violent incidents including assassinations and robberies. They were formed in the early 1970s and continued until the early 1980s. The Red Brigades attempted to create a revolutionary state through armed struggle. They also wanted to remove Italy from NATO. I said "wow" that sounds really interesting.

I told Avner that at Goddard College, where I attended, one Professor was in the Black Panthers, and one was in the Chicago Seven conspiracy trial. He seemed particularly interested with my contacts with well-known leftists.

On December 17, 1974, a group of Palestinian hijackers firebombed a Pan Am airliner at Rome, burning thirty-two passengers to death and injuring another forty. Then on April 11, in the northern Israeli town of Qiryat Shemona, the Fedayeen Palestinian terrorists attacked a residential building, killing eighteen people and wounding sixteen many of whom were women and children. In May of 1974, twenty-two children would lose their lives when terrorists from the Democratic Popular Front took them hostage in the northern Galilee town of Maalot. So this was what was going on around me at this time.

My time working in what was known as the Department Oriental was almost of a religious nature. I was studying Biblical images there, by making drawings of the objects and then integrating them into my original art. At night, I continued my reading on the Old Testament. I already understood the different books of the Torah coming from different time periods. I was most interested in the miracles that occurred. I spent a lot of time thinking about the meaning of the burning bush.

Eric Van Danekin, a German writer, had come out with a book called *Chariots of the Gods*. His hypothesis was that the burning bush on top of Mount Sinai was Moses' encounter with unidentified flying objects, UFOs, aliens from another planet. He said in his wildly popular books that the ball of fire by night and the cloud by day that led the Jews out of Egypt, was not God but alien space ships. The author said that all the miracles in the holy books could be explained by alien visitations.

I told Avner I also worked at Montmartre making money weekends and summers. He said I may see you there. He liked artists. He told me I was lucky I was American because I had freedom to travel. I could go to countries that he couldn't. On another day he brought a guy who was about ten years older than him. He looked like an ex-soldier with an Intelligent face. He and Avner had *joie de vie*. This other guy just seemed real smart. They seemed to be knowledgeable about all the things I liked - art, religion, archeology, mysticism, current events, rock and roll, etc. The other guy whose name was Uzi told me his hobby was sports and jazz music.

The next day when I saw Avner, I asked him who that guy was. Avner asked why? I said he looked like someone who was very successful and Avner responded "sometimes he freelances at my company." He said I could maybe find out who he was in the future. Avner was not the kind of man who you would think would take someone's life. He looked like a philosopher or art critique.

I would work in the Louvre Monday through Friday and for about two weeks Avner would come and talk. Weekends, I would work at Montmartre sketching tourists. Cindy and I were enjoying Paris. I was in total bliss. We were getting along really well. I was so hyper because I was so happy. I thought I could explode. We were being exposed to so much culture.

Some evenings in good weather, we would leave our apartment on the right bank and we would walk with our small son to The River Seine.

We would cross a bridge to Ile Saint Louis. Ile Saint Louis is one of the two natural islands in the River Seine. The island is named after King Louis the IX of France. The island is connected to the rest of Paris through bridges to both banks of the River. Formerly it was used for the grazing of market cattle and the stocking of wood. It's one of France's finest examples of urban planning. It was built in the seventeenth century during the reigns of Henri IV and Louis the XIII. It is a peaceful oasis of calm in the busy Paris center. Today it is an upper-class enclave with some restaurants and galleries.

We then would walk towards the Notre Dame Cathedral. The Notre Dame de Paris is French for Our Lady of Paris. It is a historic Roman Catholic Marian Cathedral located on the eastern half of Ile de la Cite in the fourth arrondissement. It is widely regarded as the finest example of French Gothic architecture and one of the largest and most famous churches in the world. It's Cathedral Treasury houses the purported Crown of Thorns and a fragment of the true cross and one of the holy nails used in the crucifixion of Jesus Christ. Its construction began in 1163 into 1240s.

We would then proceed to Boulevard Saint Michelle, one of the two major streets in the Latin Quarter. The other was Boulevard Saint Germaine. Boul Mich, as it is known in French slang, is a tree-lined street which runs south from Pont Saint Michelle on the River Seine. As the center of the Latin Quarter, it has long been a hotbed of student life and activism. When we were there in the early 1970s, it was an area with a lot of bars, music clubs and bookstores.

We got our son into a prestigious bi-lingual Montessori School which was located in the Ecliese American. The American church in Paris was the first American church established outside the United States in1814, when American Protestants started worshipping together in different homes around Paris. It is located at the present site at 65 Quay d'Orsay in the seventh arrondissement. Metro Invalides is the closest stop.

Cindy got a part time job hand coloring old French etchings. She did that for a Parisian art dealer. She had several years of French in high school and was better at speaking French than me.

I also hung around the Ecole des Beaux arts, an influential Art School in Paris. It is located in the Cartier Latin next to the Ecole des Medicine on Rue de Bonapart. Its origins go back to1648 when the academy was founded by Cardinal Mazarin to educate the most talented students in drawing, painting, sculpture, engraving, and architecture.

Louis XIV selected graduates from the school to decorate the royal apartments at Versaille. To see Marie Antoniette's bedroom with all the gold leaf is a sight to behold. In 1883, Napoleon III gave the school independence from the government.

I asked to sit in on classes at the cours des van where I had the opportunity to work doing nudes from live models. When I was a student there, it was common procedure for students to confront the teachers in a loud abusive manner in front of the class. This was something that became prevalent because of all the student demonstrations and protests. As a result of the 1960s and radical student uprisings, the students had more power. This class was basically a figure drawing class. It was in a large square room with high ceilings. There were bleacher like benches on different levels around the room. There was a platform in the center where the model would pose. It was also a great place to begin liaisons with women who might be sitting next to you.

The Ecole des Beaux classrooms were positioned around a large courtyard in the center. There were stairways up to a second level. All the ceilings were painted in trompe l'oeil decorative motives. My second favorite studio was the weaving atelier. You could build your own loom there and many threads colored with natural dies were provided for free. The Ecole des Beaux Arts School was even more interesting than the Louvre. You could go from the many different studios and see art work done from artists from all over the world.

Most or a lot of the world renowned art galleries were in that neighborhood in the Cartier Latin. Interspersed amongst the galleries, were chic home furnishing shops or small bistros and coffee shops. We mostly made friends with other artists from foreign countries. The mood on the street was very anti-American. The Vietnam war had died down. The French were against American involvement there. Hardly anyone liked Americans.

There was also a lot of anti-Israeli and anti-South African sentiment. South Africa then was white minority rule. I remember once we were told not to buy produce in the market that came from South Africa. That was because white minority rule was very unpopular. In South Africa, white immigrants, who were in a minority, had control of the government and had implemented what was known as apartheid where the Africans had to live in what were essentially ghettos. That's what it was like on the street. The mood was very political.

Socialist ideas were the order of the day. English speaking countries like England or Australia, New Zealand, and Canada were usually friendlier and easier to get to know. The anti-American sentiment could come from more of the European or Arab countries. A lot of Russians or Eastern Europeans were also nicer. The ones from the Communist countries were less anti-American.

Other countries were acting out mostly in Paris. They were setting off bombs for various reasons. France would let them in because they had a tradition of taking in those fighting for liberty. Half the country was socialist and the other half right wing, anti socialist or communist. France was having a lot of its own problems.

Many of the bombs going off were internal about France. The other bombs were political outsiders . . . could be a black liberation movement, an Algerian movement, a right wing Nazi fascist movement. People were acting out on the street nonstop. For many students and anarchists, the bombs were a form of entertainment. The groups would collaborate with each other. Various networks were established through the Universities to facilitate that.

Billy Selesnick

BILLY DRAWING PORTRAITS AT MONTMARTRE IN 1975

On a Friday night, PLO bad guys would sell gasoline to different groups who wanted to start trouble. So this is what is going on all around us. Some of the young artists I was meeting were following these kinds of events and some were not. However, everybody was effected by it.

Money was always a problem, and I depended on the income from Montmartre to feed my family. Cindy had also taken on sewing work for an interior decorator.

Montmartre is a hill in the north of Paris It is one hundred and thirty meters high. Historically, it was known as the art center of Paris. It is also a nightclub district.

On the top of the hill is the Basilica of the Sacre Coeur. This dome is a highly visible landmark. This is where artists would set up their easels to paint. Many famous artists such as Picasso, Toulouse-Lautrec and

Memoirs of an Artist

Van Gogh got their inspiration from this area; Salvador Dali, Claude Monet, Amedeo Modigliani, and Piet Mondrian did as well.

There are many sets of stairs leading to the top of this hill. There is also a Funicular railway which can take you to the top. I started working there weekends and in the summer. After a year I would vary my routine, according to my mood. When I got tired of working in the Louvre I would work at Montmartre.

Down to the southwest is the red light district of Pigalle. It was what it sounded like - Pig and alle. There were many muscular transvestites in that area. The original Moulin Rouge Theater is in Pigalle. "Moulin Rouge" was about the life and lost loves of painter Henri De Toulouse Lautrec. His claim to fame was painting prostitutes or "women of the night," as he used to call them.

It was very competitive at Montmartre. There were knife fights amongst the artists over clients. The area, at the time, was controlled by an artist mafia. They did not want any new artists. On my first day, this very kind Yugoslavian man said I could sit next to him and he would protect me. I would come up the hill weekends and also in warm weather. You could stay late and work until the wee hours of the morning.

As I made friends I had my own group to hang with and would not get hassled by what we called the sharks. The artists who worked up there were divided into different groups. There were the painters, who set up in rows and, for the most part, did mass produced paintings of local scenes. They did either the Sac le Cour or the view of Paris from Montmartre. That was awesome because Montmartre was on a mountain overlooking Paris. Some would paint the windmill at Moulin Rouge or paintings of old men smoking a pipe.

Billy Selesnick

Ninety percent was mass produced schlock. It was not about doing good art, it was about making money.

There was another group which was the portrait artists. Some sat in rows, and then others wandered and solicited tourists as they sat around the many cafes that were situated around this park.

The artists who wandered and did the portraits standing up made the most money. That's because they could get around more. There were also guys going around doing silhouettes with a scissors. They would go right up to a tourist and start cutting out a profile silhouette without the tourist's permission, and finish in about ninety seconds with a flair. It was popped into a matted cardboard frame and handed to the tourist. The artist would then charge a high price. A lot of time artists would gang up on tourists and demand very high prices. This was what would bring up the French Police (le Flic).

A lot of the roving artists would do the same thing. A common practice would be for a group of us to descend on a family and surround them. We would all be drawing them at a feverish pace. Then we would demand big bucks and scare the family into paying us. This caused friction with the artists that sat in the rows and waited for a customer. We would ravage the tourists as they got off their tour buses. They were picked clean by the time they reached the rows.

Then there was the artist mafia who decided who was going to be allowed to work there. Some were French, some Yugoslavian, some Italian. They wore expensive suits and their hair was slick. Most of them were built like football players. They also were real gigolos, who were abusive to women.

My friends were mostly guys my age, who smoked hash after a hard day's work, rather than booze. They were guys who had a leftist outlook, but were not violent or law breaking other than the hash thing.

Nobody I knew, who smoked cannabis cared that drug profits funded terrorism. There was a lot of tension between artists and there were a lot of different political persuasions there. It was bomb free. That's because it had a reputation as a playground. My friends were Scottish, British, Australian, Polish and some American.

Many of the artists there came from countries where being an artist could land you in jail. For example, I knew a Cuban artist who had a hard time getting out. He did some time for making a funny portrait of Fidel.

There was an Armenian with a scar across his throat; he had spent some time in a Russian prison. He slashed some guy with a knife that looked at him the wrong way. He then spent a year in a French nut house before they let him come back to work at Montmartre. There were artists from communist countries who had a time and a half getting out. My group was easier going. We liked smoking weed or hash and then getting laid. I was the one with the secret life. I developed a reputation as a guy in the know, who bought and sold information on the side.

SELF PORTRAIT

English was the second language there. You made more money there if you spoke English.

Artists from all over the world worked there and that could be a volatile mix. Some were hard core right wing and some were hard core left wing. When you throw money and alcohol and drugs into it, it makes for a volatile mix. The fights were always about who got the client. There was a lot of price cutting going on.

Montmartre was a place to play. Mostly all the married artists had women on the side. They kept secret apartments up there. Women came from all over Europe and the world to have a fling with an artist. Many were secretaries from Germany or Holland who came to Montmartre to party. On many occasions there were close calls with women and Cindy. Once, I was in one of these booths in a back room. It was me with another artist and two babes we were drawing for free, yet hopeful for sexual favors. Another artist rushed into the back room. He parted the curtain of our booth and told me Cindy was there with my son Joshua and she was looking all over for me. I made a quick getaway.

I was able to quench my thirst for painting big beautiful women. Although there were few stout ladies in Paris. The majority came from the farmland in Germany. I was crazy about the ones that would come with the leather shorts and suspenders. A cute one I painted had those on and a fedora hat. The smell of salt water, beer and sauerkraut would have made Rubens proud.

There were these cafes around the square. And in the square, there were rows of artists. In the cafes were the back rooms. Some had different sized booths and small theaters. I looked like Jesus Christ Super Star with long dreads and a beard that smelled like fermented cheese, and I was fighting the women off.

Montmartre was also a place where there were a lot of pickpockets. In the back rooms of the cafes that surround the Place de Tetre there were high stakes gambling with French and European organized crime figures. You could buy a gun there, get laid, or watch a sex show with animals.

The French plain-clothed Police in Paris, "Le Flic,"

were always patrolling and checking everybody's papers. If you had papers you could relax. When they would card you they would say "Papiers" (, si vous plait. If you did not have them, you were thrown into a police van and c'est la vie. I knew artists who survived for years without papers. They were some of the artists who sat quietly in the rows waiting for potential customers. They would attract less attention. They were careful. I started out without the proper papers. However, in my case, I had an American passport and a card des Jour. The problem was I needed my profession stamped in there. My profession was Artist. I went to an agency that basically certifies you are a professional tax paying artist. Then you pay tax and are allowed to work there.

The problem was that a lot of tourists were complaining of being harassed by aggressive artists, so the police imposed a rule. The tourist can ask you, but you cannot ask them. In another words, we had to sit silently and wait for the customer to speak first. The police would pose as tourists and would arrest any artists who did not go by the rules. If you had your papers, they just gave you tickets for harassing tourists, a small fine. If you did not have papers, you were deported. They just did not give you a ticket. What they did was put us in a French paddy wagon and makes us wait until it was full. Then they took us to the station and one at a time would release us. If you got picked up, it was a four- hour event.

So, between the police and the artist mafia, coming to work was like entering a jungle or a prison with babes.

Speaking of women, there were many female artists working there as well. The pretty ones who dressed sexy, would get a lot of portrait commissions. I could, if I really pushed, make five hundred dollars

U.S. in eight hours. Some made over one thousand US a day.

Some, the shy ones, made nothing. It was dog eat dog.

I got threatened once by this big Afghanni guy. He said I cut his price and he called me a Jew. This one unattractive British woman hated our clique because she was a purist, and she did not like it because we spoke English. She put a bag of rotten grapes on my chair so when I sat down I got it all over my pants and rear end.

The crowds were large there. I made many friends. After work we would score some hash, Paris style and relax. The place to go for hash (in French hash was called shit) was near a metro stop called Bellville. It's poor. It's mostly North African workers. In 1974 it looked like an Arab slum. The streets there were like winding alleyways. On one side of the street there were shops where old Arab men were smoking water pipes. On the other side of the street were North African Jewish restaurants. There were mosques and poor synagogues.

The problems of the Middle East were manifesting in the poor neighborhoods of Paris. Some of the synagogues had machine gun nests in their turrets. It looked a little to me like East Jerusalem. So when there were demonstrations on the West Bank in Israel, there would be trouble in Bellville. A lot of the French were anti Israel because the wars in the Middle East were fought in the streets of Paris. So sometimes in the early evening I would patrol the street looking for teenagers who were selling hash (shit). Nobody knew what to make of me. I had dreaded afro hair and a long beard. I wore an old raincoat and sneaks. Sometimes my family and I would have dinner in that area.

That neighborhood was torn down and concrete affordable housing blocks have been built there. It was walking distance to Pere Lachaise, Paris's largest most visited cemetery. This famous cemetery was where Jim Morrison was buried, as well as Chopin.

Smoking hash and reading about mysticism was a perfect way to spend the evening when we did not go out. I had shipped over many books from the states on biblical scholarship. At this point, I was wrestling with which books were included in the Torah and which books were excluded by whom and why. Some bible editions had more stories then others. Some bibles had different versions of the same stories. Why was that? I understood that several hundred years after the death of Jesus Christ, a conference was held of religious leaders in the Middle East. The capitol of the Roman Empire had been moved from Rome to Constantinople in Turkey. The World and religion was lead by men not by God. These men now had their own agenda. It was rebutting Mary Magdalene was Jesus' wife. They changed her to a prostitute. Their agenda was about power and control.

At a religious conference, decisions were made about which holy writings were in and which ones were out. All the best books never made it in. One such book which was written by early Christians, did not make it in this group which was liberal sexually. As a matter of fact, they believed that prayer and communion with God could be made while in sexual communion with another person of the opposite sex. This book was not chosen by the religious leaders because they wanted to exercise control over the flocks of worshippers. Other books were banned from being included in the canon, because as the result of including certain books more power or equal rights were given to women. The church was a way to keep people down and exercise control. These were things I was interested in at the time and would influence my development as an artist.

    I was always looking for interesting places to paint. I heard about this place in Paris called the Catacombs. The Catacombs of Paris are an underground ossuary. It's located south of the former city gates at metro Denfert-Rochereau. This ossuary holds the remains of six million people. It fills renovated caverns and tunnels that formerly were the remains of Paris' stone mines. In the late eighteenth century, these underground caves became a tourist attraction. It had miles of underground tunnels. Actually, when the catacombs expanded in the 1800's they moved several cemeteries to this underground location.

    I was a frequent visitor and started a series based on the catacombs. When I would go down to paint I would wear this big red cape. It was perfect to steal the skulls and hide them under my cape. I then set up mini-catacombs in our apartment and I was able to work from that.

    One Saturday morning, shortly after getting to know Avner, Cindy, Joshua and I decided to walk to Shakespeare and Company, a famous bookstore in the left bank. Shakespeare and Company is the name of two independent bookstores in Paris' left bank. It was first opened in 1919 by Syvia Beach at eight Rue de la Dupuytren, before moving to a larger property at twelve Rue de la Odeon in the sixth arrondissement in 1922. During the 1920's it was a gathering place for such writers as Ernest Hemmingway, James Joyce, Ezra Pound, and Ford Maddox Ford. It closed in 1940 and never reopened.

    The second store located at Rue de la Bucheris opened in the fifth arrondissement in 1951. Its new owner was George Whitman, son of the famous writer

Walt Whitman. There was a reading room upstairs. It also was a crash pad for wayward Americans.

Paris was a center for many exiled political groups. Many were left wing, some were right wing and some were Muslims. The French media, such as papers like Liberation, supported many leftist causes with links to terrorism. Carlos the Jackal from Venezuela was a folk hero in Paris to some. He was setting off bombs and killing innocent people including women and children. He had the reputation as a playboy and womanizer. He had sex with females who worshipped him. Carlos was born Illich Ramirez Sanchez, a Venezuela citizen. He is currently serving a life sentence in France for the 1975 murder of two French counter intelligence agents. While in prison, he was convicted of attacks in France that killed twelve people and injured another one hundred and fifty people. Avner met him when he was undercover at a hippie commune in the left bank a year before. Avner was posing as a member of the Red Brigades. Legend has it that Carlos knew where some of the people were that were on Avner's list.

In a combined operation with the Popular Front and the Japanese Red Army, Carlos set off a bomb at Le Drug Store, a popular pharmacy on the Champs Elysses, killing two people and wounding twelve. That happened when we were there. He also worked with various Palestinian groups murdering people in cold blood. He drank expensive champagne and ate expensive French food. He wore expensive hand tailored suits.

A committed Marxist Leninist, he is regarded as the most famous political terrorist of that era. He joined the Popular Front for the Liberation of Palestine in 1970. Even the most right wing warriors in Israel never targeted women and children. I was an

American with left wing leanings, but I supported Israel. I supported Labour rather then Likud.

We reached the bookstore and we went upstairs to the reading room. It had a lot of books by

Karl Marx and Che Guevara and Ho Chi Minh.

The place was swarming with students. There were several young Fidel look-alikes- beards, sandals, red scarves, army fatigues. There were half a dozen variations on Che.... short ones, tall ones. You name it. There was even a Che midget. There were also several Ho's. Some of the woman, who smelled dirty, had hairy arm pits, sandals, and babies in knapsacks. They reeked of upper class French wealth. One had a goat and monkey in tow. Washed hair was considered "de classe." It was a place where Carlos had a lot of sympathizers. These students seemed to have sympathy with the terrorist acts that were going on worldwide.

There was another couple there our age. He had long hair, wore a black leather coat, and looked friendly. He looked like a good looking rock star. He had the build of a medium height NFL line backer.

His girlfriend was tall, attractive, and looked like a hippy chick. She wore a tie-dyed skirt ankle length, and a flowered low- cut shirt showing cleavage. She had on a hat that Grace Slick or Janis Joplin could have been wearing. We started talking in English. They were Israeli and it seemed like they wanted to make friends. They both had their hair dyed the same color, henna. It was popular then.

When it was time to give them our addresses it was real weird. They both eagerly pulled out these pads and small pencils. It looked rehearsed. I thought, wow, they looked like spies. It was like why would two laid back, rock star hippies have matching small pads and short pencils. Why would they pull them out like six guns simultaneously, so eager?

It was Steve, at least that was his name in George Jonas' book. Steve and Avner were part of the original group secretly commissioned by Golda Meir. They, the couple, had followed us there. After I met Avner in the Louvre I was under surveillance. I was being watched because I had asked him for a job. Avner was interested in me because I had a lot of left wing contacts. They thought I had good left wing connections through Goddard College. At the time I did not connect it to Avner. I just thought it was a coincidence that I was meeting so many Israelis.

Steve and Yael came over the next day for a visit. I thought it was social. They were interested in what I was doing at Goddard and I showed them my pencil copies of Old Masters' paintings and my drawing of biblical artifacts. After I told them that a lot of leftists and radicals worked at Goddard, that's all they wanted to talk about. Steve seemed real tense, like he was always ready to freak out. I would tease him and say, Are you in the Mossad? He said I had a big imagination, that they were both part time students learning French. Then I would say that I always dreamed about being an agent, and he would laugh. He said he had heard that when working for the Mossad you do it for ideology and there is no pay. He also said Mossad was extremely anti drug. We had just finished smoking a joint. He said he wanted to come over alone tomorrow when Cindy was not around. I thought he wanted to go to a bar and look for women.

Salameh was the number one terrorist responsible for Munich. He was number one on the list. Salameh was wealthy and had been educated at the Sorbonne. Salameh was distantly related to Arafat. He was described as being wildly handsome and irresistible to women. He was an upper class Palestinian, whose father Sheikh Salameh had been an active fighter against Jews before the creation of Israel. He was killed by the Haganah bomb in 1948. One of his closest friends in Paris had been Mohammed Boudia who had been a member of the communist party since 1950. Avner and Steve had already killed Boudia.

He came the next day and started to ask me if I cheated on Cindy? He seemed real curious. Then he starts asking me if I had had homosexual experiences. He was very aggressive. I sensed he was looking for something with which to blackmail me. Finally, he let up. He seemed real tense. It was then that I suspected he was some sort of agent. I had heard that people involved in espionage would sometimes look for sexual information to black mail you with.

He came back the next day when Cindy was home. Yael was with him. She said they were looking to buy information? I was puzzled and said what kind. She said information about antiwar groups, Black Panthers, things like that. She said they could pay. I said I would help if I could, but truthfully, that was out of my league. I was basically a naive leftist pothead that supported Israel. Most leftists were against Israel and supported the PLO.

I did not understand it, but I was now a rogue agent in the Mossad. I was preparing for my first mission. I did not take a bath for a week. I wanted to smell French. Next was my nom de guerre. Every agent had a nick name. I stayed awake for a week and settled on two names. One was Noodles and the other was Machuga.

I asked around at Montmartre. I did not understand the enormity of my mission. I was unable to process the little information that I had gotten from Steve and Yael. I knew that they were part of the Mossad but they never were specific about Munich at that time. At first I thought it never went anywhere. The only thing it did was to enhance my reputation as an international agent and ladies man, and seeker of Rubenesque women. There were ramifications. I talked to artists from almost every country in the world. Some insisted on what kind of information I was looking for. Some wanted to know how much it paid.

    I checked out a lot of the women artists and made a point to work my other two jobs. One was to get phone numbers and the other was to get a few portraits or commissions to do nudes. The artists at Montmartre were basically a microcosm of the world. The majority was left leaning, but few supported radical PLO. There were a few Jewish artists there. I would never consider it anti-semitic. Most artists did not care about politics. They were there to make money.

    I already had a reputation at the Place. That's what we called Montmartre, Place de Theatre. My reputation was not of a frivolous playboy, but a serious artist who had some international connections. I already was getting small amounts of hash for members of my clique, from which I made a few dollars on the side.

    I was not even Parisian, but knew the streets better than some of the French artists. I had a thing for being a spotter. A spotter was someone who could finger or recognize somebody, usually a dealer, pimp, pick pocket or hit man agent. Maybe it was my ability to draw faces that gave me an edge, both in getting laid and finding out information. I had drawn by this time thousands of people. When you do someone's portrait and tell them to look you in the eye, you begin to get vibrations from people after a while. I would know things about you. I would have intuitions about people. I was part psychic part psychologist and part artist. I would purposely put people off guard by using the

Howard Hughes homeless look. People thought I was a typical starving artist. They probably did not realize that I was an artist hustler.

I think, with the Israelis, I had a reputation as someone who played both sides but my loyalty was with the Israelis. After all, I was a Jew with emotional ties to Israel. But I hung out with the enemy. The enemy being leftists or hash smokers.

Yael and Steve wanted to come back tomorrow. I thought it all seemed too weird. I thought they were junior Mossad agents on scholarship in Paris to learn French. I had no idea he was part of a rogue hit team. The next day Yael asked if she could take pictures of my writing I was doing for Goddard. I said okay. She wanted to show it to one of her friends and maybe it would lead to a teaching job in Israel. She pulled out this miniature camera to take pictures of my notes. She also bought a drawing from me. She was real insistent on getting a certain kind of receipt.

Steve told me about his friend in Germany who had an antique store. He wanted to get my art in there. He always talked about his friend and I was already packed. We were talking about a giant one- man show. I thought his name was Hans but I'm not sure. I just knew I was having a one man show in Germany. Actually, Steve and I were planning to go there by train. I remember going with him to get the tickets. We were getting them a few days in advance of our trip. I was carrying my extra big portfolio with twenty pieces of my art in it. Then something happened that went into "the box of secrets." The "box of secrets" was where I put things that happened to me that I was not able to process.

All I remember is that we were walking down the street, and I heard the sound of what I thought was a car muffler back-firing. Steve grabbed my arm in a rough manner and dragged me away. The next thing I knew we were having coffee in a café. Steve told me that someone took a shot at us. It's a noisy city. Someone takes a shot with a .22 caliber firearm with a silencer. Nobody even notices. Maybe you would hear a ping and it's like a small pebble hits a concrete wall. Someone tried to kill us. Steve and I were targets of an assassination attempt. Steve was really upset and scared. It did not faze me in the least because I did not even realize it happened. I thought it was some kind of joke. Steve was wondering if we would make it home. We split up there he went his way and I went my way. I was concerned but not really worried or scared. I just could not process it.

When I got home and told Cindy, she asked, "what were you smoking"? Either way, some kids in a hot rod took a shot at us. It was a politically motivated assassination attempt.

Salemeh was an obsession with Avner and Steve because he was number one on their list. He was generally regarded as the man responsible for the murder of the Israelis in Munich. Steve hinted around that he had a job to do and he wanted to go home.

Steve and Yael began coming over every day. Then one day Steve came in real upset. His friend in Germany, who owned the antique shop, died a mysterious death. This was a member of the team who was murdered by a Palestinian reprisal squad. Then the next day Yael came over without Steve and told us some things.

She said Steve was involved in things that were really dangerous, and she was upset about it. On some visits, Steve was very angry and made threatening comments to me. I still would tease him about being a Mossad agent and I said I wanted to join. I was kidding around. He said there was a strict policy that no one gets in who smokes hash or takes drugs. After all, they were looking to buy information. I mean I knew some things. I did not know that they were after the terrorists that were responsible for killing the Israelis at Munich.

Eventually he hinted around that he worked for someone who was known as the" Old Man," and that he was a revered figure. He said one day I may get to meet him. I had to be patient. Steve said it could happen when I least expect it. It would not be an appointment or interview; it would not happen like that. Steve was very mysterious about it. This was going to be a job interview. A step up the ladder.

We had spent a few days planning a very important new mission. We were going to tell people we were in a rock band and try to meet left wing hippies or people in the French underground. I had long hair and a long beard. I usually wore a biblical cap and an old rain coat with red sneakers. I did not want to be noticed. I looked like I was just run over. We would then bring them back to our place to see if we could figure out their politics.

Yael had the Grace Slick, Joan Baez look - totally beautiful. Long hippy skirt tie dyed, Rock and roll hat. She was tall. Joan Baez and Grace Slick were two famous female rock stars. Steve was all decked out in black leather.

We went out on this mission and met some weird looking student underground types and brought them back to our place. We smoked some hash. Steve was trying to figure out if these people had any contact with the PLO. Steve was beginning to get inpatient. They stayed the afternoon. It was not fruitful. Yael thought our plan had potential, but needed refining. We were going to try it again the next day but things happened.

Later that afternoon, after Steve and Yael left, I was out for a walk with Cindy and my son. A small French looking hot rod pulled up real fast and these men jump out. It was three young men in their late teens early twenties with olive complexions. There was also a fourth man with them who acted as if he was their boss. He was a rough looking heavy set man with black curly hair and bad skin who was older.

    I had my art with me and I began to show them. I said I was a socialist Jew from America. They admired my art and made some comments about my Zionist friends and that they were looking for them and then took off. One of the teenagers had a crazy look in his eye. The look of someone who took pleasure in killing. I got a vibe that he thought killing was the ultimate way out deed.

    I told Steve the next day. He said they were the guys that took a shot at us on the way to the train station. I drew a portrait of their ring leader from memory. He said that soon I would meet his boss known as the Old Man. Steve said I was in deep now.

    A few days later, I went to the souk to score hash. The word "hashish" is actually derived from the word "assassin." They were a cult who killed for Mohammed around 800A.D. Most hash in Paris was from the Bekka Valley in Lebanon. It funded PLO terrorist projects.

    When I scored, I noticed it was the PLO hit dudes, and they said I could get bulk at a better price. I told them even though I was a Jew, I was a committed leftist and I got high. For the time being they seemed interested in getting Steve and not me. These PLO dudes did not hate all Jews; you got a pass if they made money off of you. You also had a second pass if you were socialist.

    I told them to come up to Montmartre and we could talk. So this PLO terrorist hash dealer comes to sell me hash in bulk. When this dude, who I nicknamed Big Daddy, came to sell me hash, some

Memoirs of an Artist

guys from the Mossad who were watching me, came along and whisked him off. We had been preparing for this operation for a few days. We had rehearsals where different Isreali agents would prepare me for the day of the operation. He was taken to the dump outside of Paris. So far, I had been shot at and then complicit in flushing out my would-be assassin. I was asked if I wanted to go for a ride to the dump that was on the outside of Paris. I have a vague recollection of the small car.

I told Steve, who was at Montmartre that day, and he said I was really in now and I could possibly be in danger. Then one day he came over and admitted he was a Mossad man. He said he was investigating me and he concluded that I was no threat to the state of Israel. He then said, if I see him around town at cultural events, I was to ignore him. He also said if I ever wrote anything about Israel, no matter where I lived, he would find me and do me in. I thought," what did I do," he was being dramatic. I just said okay because I knew he had a short fuse. When someone threatens to kill you it has a way to make you forget certain things. At least it did for me.

Then he informed me that his investigation of me was being handed over to someone else. I told him I thought I was being followed. I just thought I was meeting a lot of Israelis who seemed to be agents. After that we did not see each other as much. We did not have a phone and they never gave me their number. I started to see Avner again at the Louvre. He informed me he was going to be traveling a lot between his apartments. I would see him when he would be around.

In 1974, the year that I had met Steve, three unidentified Arabs were shot in a church near Glarus, Switzerland. Glarus is located in the heart of Switzerland. There is also a lot of snow there. Their target was Salameh. He was there for a meeting with Abu Daoud. Avner and Steve walked in on their three armed bodyguards and shot them. They had to abort because they were about to be discovered. Salameh and Abu Daoud were supposed to meet in the church on Saturday, January12. Avner and Steve never got them. So, when a little time went by and I did not see Steve, that's what he was doing.

Steve told me that one day in the future I may have a mental breakdown when I find out what he was doing. He said I would feel that I was run over by a truck and he would not be able to help me. He strongly hinted of an epiphany in the future. There was so much deception.

Cindy and our son went back to New Jersey for a month and I was on my own. I said I needed the space to finish my Masters studies with Goddard. We all lived in one small room and sometimes we would get on each other's nerves.

When she was gone I wanted to save money. My goal was rather then shop and pay for groceries, I was going to try to beat the system. When the markets closed I would go through the garbage and look for food that was thrown away. I could find a few bruised potatoes, a few old turnips or carrots. The ones the rats had not gotten yet. After some practice I got good at it and knew where to find the best garbage. I would take it home and make stew. I wanted to see if I could live off the land like being in the old west. I was doing my art then all the time. I would work at the Louvre, go to the Beaux Arts and then work at Montmartre.

My relationship with Cindy was still okay even though she was away. We just needed space. You know what they say, familiarity can breed contempt.

I met a hot chick at the Beaux Arts Academy where I was drawing nudes. I went to a dinner with her at her sister's house. This was when Cindy and my son were away. They had left wing street credibility because her sister lived in a very rough neighborhood.

My new woman friend was named Dominique. I sat next to her at the Beaux Arts. Thin and tall, she wore blue jeans with holes in the right places. Long curly wild hair with a large sensual mouth. She was the first women I met who refused to call Israel its name because it had no right to exist. She referred to it as Palestine. She then said her boyfriend was a photographer and worked in Beirut. She was a French Hanoi Jane with bedroom eyes. I pretended to be sympathetic to her views, but inwardly, although a leftist, I was not so on Israel.

At dinner her sister recounted a month long camel ride in the desert of Morocco.

It was rough being American. Every political group hated us. Then, if you were a left wing Jew, even more people want to be rude to you, including faux Fidels.

Back then I thought I could convert her to my cause through great love making. She also became my connection for a new variety of hash from India. It was called hash oil. Apparently many left wingers in Paris had open marriages. I got to meet her husband and he refused to speak much English. I pretended to understand what he was saying in French when he was calling me a sleaze bag, and then he threatened to kill me if I did anything that was not appropriate with his girlfriend.

I had dinner with Dominique and I was on the way home on a bus when I saw a man staring at me and smiling. He looked about mid fifties, glasses, and he wore this cap which made him look like a spy. He was short. He looked very Eastern European. I was uncomfortable being stared at. I got off the bus and he followed. I stood on the corner and we were both looking at the bus map on a kiosk. I turned to him and said shalom. He tensed up. I tried French; he looked startled. Then in English I said I was sorry I thought you were Israeli. He looked at me and said where are your parents? I said my father was in the south of France and lived there with my mother. I told Gideon that he was a successful business man who was in the dry cleaning business. Then he asked me, "who I was working for"? I said I was an art student in Paris. He asked again, "who do you work for"" I was confused but sensed this was the old man that Steve told me about.

I asked why he was following me and he said that I penetrated his security wall. We talked for over an hour right there in the street. He asked me what I believed in and I said world peace. He was annoyed by that and said I was naïve. He asked me if I heard about what happened in Munich in 1972. I said I had and it was awful. He asked me what I would think if he told me he was hunting down terrorists and bringing them to justice. Then Gideon starts asking me if I was writing a book, perhaps a book about espionage. I said no. Then he asked me if I was going to write a book in the future. I said if I did I hope it would be about my art. I then said I would not write anything about Israel. That was not my intention. Then he asked me if I had the outline for a book and I said no. Then he said that there was a Jewish writer in Israel that was in jail for writing a book about espionage and that he had crossed the line and was now doing time in a Israeli prison.

I was in disbelief but went on with the conversation. He then started making accusations that I was part of the new left and that was hostile to Israel. I said check me out. I love Israel and my father gives a lot of money to the UJA. He said he would, and pulled out this small pad and pencil. It looked like he got it at the same store as Steve and Yael.

Memoirs of an Artist

He then asked me if Steve was too aggressive with me. I said I did not like being accused of being a homosexual.

Little did I know that Gideon was not only a heroic legend, but was chief of Mossad. Gideon was born in Poland in 1925. He immigrated to Israel when he was a year old. He was a major general in the Israeli defense forces and director of the Mossad between 1968 and 1974. During his tenure, he helped carry out Operation Wrath of God, the Israeli response to the Munich massacre. And he was personal friends with Golda Meir and Ariel Sharon.

I believe that he felt that because I was anti-war, smoked pot, loved rock and roll and had leftist sympathies that I was an unwilling pawn of the Kremlin. I told him a lot of American lefties were Jewish. Just because I read Fidel Castro's biography and dreamed of picking sugar cane on the island, that I was not his enemy. He just looked at me and said for me to follow my dreams. When I told him about my work for Goddard he said he saw it already on microfilm. Those were the pictures Yael took. Gideon gave the impression of being very smart but tough. He seemed to be also very compassionate. He was from a different generation We talked about the fact that I was married and was seeing women on the side. He asked me if I loved Cindy and my son and I said that I did. I just was incapable of processing what he was telling me. After a while talking on the street, we each went our own way. I felt our conversation was unfinished.

The next day I went to work at Montmartre. I was asking people if they wanted their portraits done. I heard someone say, Selesnick come here, I want to talk to you. It was Gideon. I said sorry I did not recognize you. He had the kind of face that blended in.

He dressed so non-descript that you would think he was invisible. He had that eastern European cap on which I thought was a dead give- away that he was a spy.

He told me then that he had an Interpol card and he could arrest me. He said that he knew everything about me and I had a connection to a drug ring.

The truth was some friends from Trenton had visited me and they did have connections. Then he said he and his friends hated guys with beards and who wore sandals. At this point I thought he was some kind of super cop and he was after me for drugs. I was not a big time drug dealer. I smoked pot and sold art to people who did. I told him that.

He said it was illegal to profit from drug dealers and that I could be jailed for it. We always would have these long philosophical conversations. We would talk about books and the subject of the book Exodus comes up. It was written by Leon Uris, he was one of my favorite writers. I had read all his books. Gideon then told me some things about Leon who he says he knows personally and then he goes on to tell me one of the characters in that book was based on him. I did not know what to think. Here I was in this incredible place (Paris) talking to this incredible man. He then asked me if I wanted to make some extra money. He might have a job for me and he was going to come back tomorrow and see me.

I was "in" now. I was almost a full-fledged secret agent. I already had more girlfriends than James Bond.

The next day I was hustling portraits and Gideon came back. We were talking and I thought we were developing a friendship. He would vacillate from being fatherly to being threatening. He said he could help me get an art show at a major museum in Israel. This was going on when I was hustling portraits at

Montmartre When Gideon was at Montmartre, there were always other agents around. We talked a lot about different philosophies. He was a fan of Ayn Rand and he brought an inscribed copy. He knew her, and she wrote a message to Gideon on the first page. I asked him if they had sex. And he said she was a very sexy woman, a sex addict.

Ayn Rand was a famous writer. She was a refugee from communist Russia. She was a militant anti communist. Her books espoused a love of capitalism. She also founded a philosophy called Objectivism. She charged for these lectures which espoused free love and a cult of selfishness. Her most famous book called "The Fountainhead" was made into a Hollywood movie.

Every day now I had jobs. These jobs were going on when I was hustling portraits from tourists. Some days my job was just to stay in one area and work. I did not know and was not told what when on in other areas. Just talking to him was like a job. He already was talking to me like my father who did not like me. A very sensitive intelligent and compassionate person, and I was working for him. I had slowly come to realize that this incredible man was like a father to all the children who fought for the state of Israel. We would have these conversations where he offered me the opportunity to come and live in Israel and perhaps in the future lead to citizenship in Israel. He said what I was doing was dangerous and he may have some bigger jobs for me. Gideon and me were always having these philosophical discussions about the hippies or underground or student protesters against the establishment. He said it was not cool to be involved with protests. For example, if you were to be involved with a protest against South Africa apartheid that the young and the restless had to wait for that racist government to be voted out by peaceful means. Gideon said it was irresponsible to do otherwise. The same thing could apply to the controversy about the war in Vietnam. He would say it was not cool to participate in any illegal protests that the young and restless should vote the war out of existence. I then asked him about the Stern gang. A saw a tear come to his eyes. You're talking about something that was really complicated.

Avraham Stern was born in 1907 in Poland. At the age of eighteen he immigrated to Israel. He attended Hebrew University where he graduated with honors in classical languages and Greek and Latin literature. He rose to become leader of a paramilitary organization called Irgun. Irgun was a Zionist organization that operated in mandate Palestine between 1931 and 1948.They believed that every Jew had a right to enter Palestine. In 1940 he formed a breakaway group called Lehi. He considered Irgun too passive in dealing with the British occupiers. In 1948 Irgun integrated into the Israeli armed forces. Sterns' group was considered extremists by Israeli mainstream. People died from all sides in his attempts to get the British out of Palestine. Avraham Stern wrote dozens of poems that expressed his sensual love for Israel and his willingness to become a martyr for his cause. He was an extremely charismatic figure. He died in a controversial shoot out in 1942. Gideon's response to the Stern gang was that people have to obey the law. He said he could understand young people's fascination in being drawn in by a charismatic figure but the law is the law. If I were young and living in Israel during that time period I would have been attracted to him to. What Abbie Hoffman, Timothy Leary Huey Newton was to me, hero out laws. To Gideon, and people from his generation, Stern could

Memoirs of an Artist

have been their hero. Stern's story was so charismatic.

He then goes on to talk about people he admired and knew. Gideon wanted me to learn about one of his friends. He spoke very highly about a man he knew who passed away in 1961. His name was Sam the Banana Man. Gideon and Sam had some history. He was referring to Sam Zemurray. Sam was born in 1877 in what is today Moldolvia. To escape pogroms he immigrated to the states, and by the time he was 21 made a small fortune selling discarded bananas in New Orleans. With that money Sam bought five thousand acres in Honduras along the Cuyamel River in 1910. At that time the government of Honduras was working to reschedule its debt. The new taxes would have put Sam out of business. So Sam Zemurray returned to New Orleans where the deposed president of Honduras was living in exile. Sam hired two mercenaries and along with the deposed president orchestrated a coup that saved Sam's business. At one time Sam owned the Cuyamel Fruit Company and later owned United Fruit Company. Gideon was also friends with Sam's grandson who was my age. He was coming to Paris and Gideon wanted me to meet him. The family was anti- communist and when Sam's grandson and I met he commented on how much I looked like Che which was not cool. He later came to visit me in my art gallery in the states.

One day Gideon asked me if I met a lot of interesting people working in Paris. I told him I did. He asked me to describe some of them. I told him I met a lot of Israelis at the Louvre. I told him I met this interesting guy named Avner. He seemed startled. He basically told me that Avner was a friend of his and had been missing meetings. He said Avner was doing secretive work that was embarrassing to the state of Israel. He reminded me that I had penetrated his

Security wall. I really was confused and went along with it.

Then he said Golda Meir was aware of me and my name was going to be brought up at their next meeting. He said I knew about things that affected the security for the state of Israel. I just stood there in disbelief. I thought he was a super cop, but this was outside the sphere of what I could comprehend. I thought Avner, Steve, Gideon were all connected somehow, but I was still in the dark about a clandestine hit squad. I know Gideon had told me when I met him but I still was unable to process it.

In 1974, the year I met Avner and Steve and the rest of the small crew, they had a meeting at a hotel in London called the Europa. There were also back up squads of Mossad agents in different cities that were there to help out. The different members of the group lived in different cities in Europe and they were often traveling to see each other. I had met some of the group but not all. I was most familiar with Avner, Steve and Gideon.

They had been there for a few days. There was a bar at this hotel called the Etruscan. A member of the team named Carl was having a drink there. There was an attractive slim blond sitting at the bar. She was in her early thirties with shoulder length hair and beautiful blue eyes. Carl, thinking she was a prostitute, struck up a conversation and before you knew it they were up in his room. Avner found him dead in bed the next morning.

Avner found out who she was and where she was from. She lived in Holland on a houseboat. To make a long story short, Avner and Steve went to her house boat in Holland, took revenge and killed her. This part of the story is in The George Jonas book and the Spielberg movie. This woman was not on their original list.

One day I wanted to score some hash. It was on the other side of town. It was hard to get to, it entailed making a lot of changes on the Metro. I left from my apartment in the first arrondissement. I felt I was being followed. My modus operandi was to confront and talk to people who I thought were following me.

This was a new hash connection and a new man who was tailing me. Gideon told me that now that I was involved he had to keep an eye on me at all times. The new hash connection was near Belleville but not in the souk. This was a street where all the people who lived there had to move because of some big building project. After the city made them move, a group of hippy drug dealers, green party members, and anarchists squatted there.

They hooked up water and electricity. They had guards at the beginning of the street. It had been raided several times but the city had yet to evict the Squatters. It was rumored to be the beginnings of an underground utopian community. It was there that I was going under surveillance.

I got my hash and was on my way home when I saw my pursuer in the shadow of a doorway. He was about thirty-five, tall, brown hair, a cap like Gideon's and wearing a raincoat. I approached and tried to speak. He seemed nervous and acted like he did not understand me. I tried English but he did not understand that either. He opened his coat and I saw he had a gun in his belt.

I thought it was time to back off. I walked slowly towards the metro with him in the shadows. After all I was holding twenty dollars worth of Hash. They called them fingers. That was the size of the hash, the shape of a finger. I made my way home. By now it was dark. When I entered my building and went up the steps I heard him behind me. I was trying not to think about it. I went in my house, smoked a hash joint and before I fell asleep I heard what sounded like mice outside my door. It was him.

The next day at Montmartre I told Gideon about it. He said the agent did not speak English and that I scared him when I tried to talk to him. I was lucky I did not get hurt. Gideon told me that he was from Hungary and had been jailed and tortured by the communists. He worked for Gideon now and was a psychotic killer. I just stared at him in disbelief, wondering what I had done. It could not be about drugs. This was too far out.

I was unofficially in the rogue Mossad. I worked at Montmartre. I studied at the Louvre. I did art work at the Ecole des Beaux Arts. And at night I studied the Jewish holy books.

My area of studies now was about the religion of idol worshipers with whom the Jewish people competed. There were idol worshipers and sub groups. Many of the premonotheistic religions had to do with nature fertility, and the growing of crops. Some of the Gods named during that period were Baal and Ashtarte.

The crops fed the people. The rain caused the crops to grow. Some ancient people believed the rain was from Baal and Astarte in heaven having sex. The rain was the climax of semen dripping down to earth. The rain was needed to feed the people. So the humans on earth below would practice fertility to get the crops to grow and get it to rain. They would have intercourse in temples during time of drought to get it to rain. There were temples found in the shape of vaginas and the priest would dress as a penis and walk through the rooms of the temple to simulate intercourse. There was an inner room representing the inner room of a women's womb. The holy man would anoint his head with oil to make penetration easier. They were sex-based religions where women working as temple prostitutes servicing the men was like fertilizing the crops.

Around this time Cindy and Joshua came back from their trip to the states. We missed each other and were glad to be back together again. I went back to Montmartre the next day. I had a family to feed. Gideon was not glad to see me and he said go home Selesnick. 1 did not know this was not about drugs, and I felt he was trying to discredit me around Montmartre.

I stayed, made a few dollars, and had my favorite drink in one of the cafes. It was French; it was called Panache – half lemonade, half beer. Great on a hot day.

I was stressed. This guy Gideon would not leave me alone and the French artist mafia was giving me a hard time. Some days Gideon was glad to see me and I had jobs; other days he acted mad at me and told me to go home.

The big guy who ran the artist mafia was like a football player. With thick dark hair, he acted like he was head of the mafia in Europe. He told people whether they were allowed to work there. Actually, he was a French Jew with an attitude. He felt the whole world was against him and his family because he was Jewish. When he first saw me up there, he would say I was not allowed to work there. There were always two or three cohorts along with him. They all wore expensive suits. When it was cold they wore expensive fur coats. His friends were Yugoslavs. He did not care that I was Jewish. He was a bully with backup. Whenever I saw him I ran. There were crowds there. Lately he was always around. During one encounter I told him my father lived in the south of France. After that he was a little nicer to me. But it was his friends, the ones in their fur coats, who were so threatening.

People always remember my last name. It's pronounced Selznick, a well known name in the movie business. David O Selznick who had made *Gone with the Wind* actually was my fifth or sixth cousin.

In 1974, word had come to Avner and Steve that Ali Hassan Salameh was supposed to arrive in the small Spanish town of Tarifa, on the Atlantic coast between Gibraltar and the Portuguese border. A young armed unidentified Arab is shot dead in a garden there.

Avner and Steve were always flying in and out of town.

Pierre, the mafia don at Montmartre, now wanted me to pay union dues. There was a mysterious break-in when we were not home. There was about five hundred dollars in a wooden box on my desk. It was gone. My papers had been checked. My letters to Goddard were all around.

On days when I went to work at Montmartre and Gideon was not there, there were other Mossad agents. There was the rogue Mossad and then the regular Mossad. One day I had just made it up about twenty flights of steps and as I entered Montmartre, there, at a table, sat a number of agents. One was very thin. He was the bookkeeper for the rogue group. He commented on the fact that I was very thin. He said all my exercise will pay off.

Goddard, according to Gideon, was a link to the Kremlin because of all the lefties we had there. American foreign policy thought that anti-war people and hippies were indirectly Russian plants. That's because those groups were starting trouble in America and in Europe. When people used to talk about the Mossad, a feeling so freaky came over me and I said I kept those feelings deep in my head in this wooden box. It was the same wooden box I kept on my desk.

THE VIEW FROM MY NEW APARTMENT

Back when my wife Cindy was away, I was seeing Dominique. I told Dominique when Cindy came back that it was over. French women thought it was okay to be friends with your wife. That's the way they did it in civilized societies. I owed her two hundred francs for some oil. I was mad at her because she stopped putting out so I was going to stiff her for the Hash oil.

She tracked me down when Cindy returned and demanded to be let in. Dominique stated she wanted to be friends with Cindy but Cindy was not into it. There was a scene between the two women and me. I paid off Dominique and that was the end of our pow wows.

We changed apartments. We found a bigger apartment for the same price. It was at seventy-five

Rue Quincompoix, a narrow charming street just west of Centre Pompidou, a famous contemporary art museum. There are many restaurants and galleries there now.

Cindy and I had met an American student, who was leaving town, at Shakespeare and Company, the left wing bookstore. She turned us on to it. She went to a college similar to Goddard. We became friendly with her. She told us her mother was really rich. Her boyfriend Phillip was also American. His father moved to Paris after World War II. He was a famous lawyer who wrote the new constitution for Germany after the war.

Our street was in the middle of a red light district. Prostitution in France was the exchange of sexual services for money. These include soliciting, procuring, or operating a brothel.

In 1946 France signed the convention for the suppression of the trafficking of person and the exploitation of the prostitution. With these moves, France has become a major supporter of the inter abolishment movement, advocating the eradication of prostitution with someone under the age of eighteen. During the Napoleonic era, France became the model for the regulatory approach to prostitution. Despite the laws, prostitution was practically legal. There was a scene on our street. There was a scene in Pigalle. There was a scene in the Bois de Boulogne. The prostitutes had unions. They had rights. They even, in Paris, had respect.

Prostitution and pornography was a very big part of espionage and the dirty wars that were fought on the streets of Paris. Every doorway on our new street had different colored women in it. You could see every color and every nationality on the face of this earth. The different outfits were, scantily dressed nurse, nude with chains, nude in a fur coat, school teachers in their underwear, or many other variations. In the summer some were nude. Sometimes you would see Lesbian sex in the doorway. You would see every variation on a psychological sexual minutia. Not too many were transvestites. That was on another street, Rumor had it the streets were paved in the days of Christ. The buildings looked it; they were markedly warped.

The whores shared the streets with the clochards. They were bums but this was Paris. Some were vets or war heroes, PhD's and mostly alcoholics.

This street was also known for its garbage. These factories were places where old cardboard was stored before being sold for bulk. The clochards had pushcarts where they would collect paper or cans. They usually slept on the floor in their shops. And so it was, the clochards and the hookers.

Going to the local bakery was different. The girls would be in line in there in their sexy outfits. One woman was nude and she was wearing a fur coat that was open. I had my young son with me a lot. They would fuss over him. They said it was the safest street in Paris because the girls watched the street.

At the butcher, there could be a stunning exotic beauty in line naked in a bikini, or full frontal with whips, chains and handcuffs, and nobody would flinch. Then there was the pierced lady with hundreds of piercings all over her body. I wonder if the butcher gave them extra sausage because they were hot. There were proper looking people in the line too.

Our apartment was a few floors above a bar. It had been designed by a French hippy architect. We had the attic top floor. It was nice, but the toilet was a hole in the floor with the foot pedals.

After work, my friends, artists from Montmartre,

would come over to Rue Qiuncompoix with their girlfriends. First we would cook a feast. Then we would smoke some hash, French style. It was called a spleef. That was when you mixed tobacco in with the hash and then roll it into a funnel shape big joint.

The boys would go for a walk leaving the girls to talk. Cindy liked the girlfriends and wives of the other artists.

We would check out the shows in the doorways. I thought that the art by Toulouse- Lautrec was awesome. We, the boys, had our portfolios with us, along with our pastels and charcoal. I wanted to do a series like Toulouse- Lautrec. Henri Marie Raymond de Toulouse Lautrec-Monfa lived from 1864 to 1901. He was a French painter, printmaker, draftsman and illustrator. His immersion in the contemporary and modern life in the 1800's yielded a lot of exciting, elegant and provocative images of the decadent life of those times. Toulouse Lautrec, along with Cezanne, Gauguin and Van Gogh, are the most well known painters of the Post Impressionist era. He came from an aristocratic family. He suffered from a congenital health condition attributed to inbreeding. He was less than five feet tall. His most well known paintings are of prostitutes from Paris.

Approaching a lady of the night, I explained in my broken French that I wanted to do paintings of her. She said follow me. I was taken to this house. The ground floor was a garbage factory with the clochards sleeping in there with their pushcarts. There were piles of cardboard and there was an area that was just cans and glass bottles. The façade had a layer of dirt that went back to the days of Christ. You got towels in the lobby, which was a side door around back from the garbage factory. You went up some narrow bent steps and at the top the doors opened and you entered into a giant playroom all decorated in very fancy furniture. It was a modern large lobby-like space with doors going into different rooms. The building was old and the floors sloped. However, it was clean. The furniture was old and it looked like it was from the period of World War Two. Music was playing over an intercom; a lot of ladies were dancing around half naked. There were card games in some rooms-strip poker. People were smoking water pipes in other rooms. It was almost like a masquerade party. In some rooms there were guys in suits smoking cigars playing cards. It was like an opera by Mozart.

My friends were with me. They split off in different directions. This plump woman in a ballerina outfit came up to me and said, "J'adore les Americans." I was glad someone liked Americans. Life was like that then in 1975 Paris art school, but Golda Meir? What's up with that?

I made friends with this cute Rubenesque one who liked Americans. I painted her many times, though never when she was with a customer. I had a puritanical streak. I gave her many of my paintings and she and I became friends. She was French. She started turning tricks when she was sixteen. Her uncle had talked her into having sex when she was twelve.

I would go to her when I drank too much beer and smoked too much hash. From time to time I got a freebie. I did not have to take my socks off. She came to visit me a few times when I was working at Montmartre.

It was convenient living on Rue Quincampoix I needed an escape from the Mossad and the artist mafia at Montmartre. To relax, I started make friends with the pimps in my neighborhood. Some nights I could not sleep. I used to go for these long walks when I had insomnia. I would explore neighborhoods that had prostitution. I would go into bars where pimps would hang out with their girls. I would observe the relationships that they had. I could have written a book about it.

My friends at Montmartre all had their own issues. Some could not get papers, some had money problems, and others had problems with women. So I never really talked about the agents or Gideon. I knew Avner, but I did not know he was a hero superstar. I just knew that Gideon was looking for Avner because he was missing meetings. There was drama going on all over. So far, Steve's friend the antique dealer died a mysterious death and then the woman who was as a prostitute was murdered. I was shot at and complicit in the disappearance of that shooter.

My favorite restaurant, Goldenberg's on Rue de Rosier, had been fire bombed by some French P.L.O. Goldenberg's was located in the heart of a district known as the Marais. I went in there a few hours after the bombing. A Molotov cocktail had been thrown in. The terrorist escaped in a car. Before the bombing you would enter and there would be salamis hanging from the ceiling. There would be barrels of pickles. There would be these two deli cases with delicious meats and other items. There would be the man going from table to table playing the violin.

That was the old Jewish quarter. It is a famous historical area. It hosts many important buildings that have historical as well as architectural importance.

The Marais is located between the third and fourth arrondissement in Paris. In 1240 The Order of the Temple built its church just outside the walls of Paris in the northern part of the Marais. The temple turned this district into an important area and many religious Institutions were built there.

This area became a favorite with the nobility.

When the nobility came it also attracted many Jewish people and it became a center for Jewish life in Paris.

The Nazis used this area as a staging ground to deport Jews. It has many stationary stores. It had boutiques that specialized in Marbleized paper or marbleized object d'art. It also had very chic home furnishing stores.

On my market street there continued to be bombings at the socialist and communist party offices. I would eat in student restaurants; there were many near the universities. They would be sponsored by different cultural organizations. The Jewish student restaurant across from Jardin des Luxemburg was bombed. Basically, there was firebombing every Friday night and between all the groups, there was at least one or two other bombings a week. I got to see most of them. It became a sort of hobby.

Every day that Gideon was not at Montmartre there were other Mossad or rogue Mossad. I could tell the difference. I would talk with them, do their portraits.

There was an American ex-marine, who told me he subcontracted; he was part of the Israeli group. He was part of the back-up group. Something the American mercenary said triggered some serious amnesia. He liked me. After we left Paris, he would somehow find my phone number. Many times I had no phone. When he called he was always drunk and crying. Some years I knew who he was. Once he made a blood and gut confession. Other times I just did not recognize his voice. I would say where do I know you from? He promised he would only call once a year because he knew he was a piece of work. Sometimes when he called he would say I know you from Paris. I said where and that I did not understand. Every call was more morbid. His wife had cancer. Then he had cancer. Then the calls stop.

What I saw in Paris was so much trauma it erased my memory. Everything was so confusing. Today I am crying because I was not there for my friend. I cannot stop the flow of tears. The American guy liked me and I was not there at his time of need. He saved me in my hour of need.

The Mossad always spoke to me cryptically and sometimes were very serious and almost menacing. The only thing I knew was that Avner was missing his meetings. They also told me one day they were all going to be superstars in the movies. They asked me if I knew what they were talking about. I said no. They said they wanted to take me with them to stardom because I was so eccentric. The American mercenary told me that. Gideon had told me that he was hunting for terrorists that were responsible for Munich. It never registered with me. Once Gideon said to me that I was lost in a blizzard, a snowstorm. He said that he did not know if I would make it back. He said it was not my fault it was happenstance. He said I did not have the training to survive. He said that if I made it back in I might end up being successful and being a millionaire. He mentioned the title called the spy who came in from the cold. There was so much deception going on.

When the hash dealer, PLO hit man who had come for a visit to Montmartre to sell me hash he had changed his appearance. He wore a fedora hat and a western looking golf polo shirt with smart looking jeans, black socks and loafers. He had on expensive sunglasses that hid his pock marked face. He looked so westernized he almost looked Jewish. His body type I describe as swarthy, heavy set. In actuality he worked and sympathized with the famous terrorist Abu Nidal. Abu Nidal was born in 1937 and lived to 2002. His name was Sabri Khalif al-Banna. He was founder of Fatah a militant Palestinian splinter group also known as the Abu Nidal organization. At the height of his power in the 1970s and 1980s he was regarded as the most ruthless of the Palestinian terrorists. He told Der Spiegel in a rare interview in 1985 that "I am an evil spirit which moves around at night causing nightmares." His movement was called the Socialist Rejectionist Front because they rejected proposals for a peaceful settlement with Israel. He split with Yasser Arafat in1974 and set himself up as a freelance contractor. Abu Nidal ordered attacks in twenty countries injuring over nine hundred people. His most notorious attack was when he bombed El Al airlines in the airport of Rome and Vienna. Arab gunmen high on amphetamines opened fire killing eighteen and wounding one hundred and twenty at the airport in Rome.

Abu Nidal was from a wealthy Palestinian family from Jaffa where they owned orchards and other businesses. He died in 2002 in Bagdad by orders from Saddam Hussein. The Iraq government said it was death by suicide. Before his death he had ordered and attempted assassinations on Yassar Arafat and Mahmoud Abbas.

The Mossad, picked him up, the PLO bad guy. I called him Big Daddy when he came up to Montmartre to sell me some hashish. They were watching him. They were watching me. That day seemed to go in slow motion. I had been prepped and trained now.

The agent that took Big Daddy down was the guy I met with Avner in the Louvre, not the old man but Avner's accomplice on another day. The one I said that had joie de vie. The one who liked sports and jazz.

Not all the agents liked me, according to the American mercenary who worked with the Israeli's.

Billy Selesnick

There was talk about doing me in because I knew too much. The guy that did the job on Big Daddy was the guy that did not like me. His name was Uzi and he told Gideon that he thought I was gay. That's about the worst insult you can endure when you are trying to fit in with a bunch of guys. I was different from most of them. I was a flower child that would wear beads and bells. I would wear weird hats. After the hash dealer assassination, Gideon told that agent to take some time off.

Even Gideon told me that that Uzi was pissed because Avner let me find out too much. Apparently, the PLO hit man was taken to a dumping ground in Paris where even the reporters don't go. I was asked to go along on that ride, but can't seem to remember. I just remember setting him up and fingering him. The dope dealing terrorist asked to call his family in the west bank, he appealed to the agents' sense of Jewishness that honored family. I have some memory of the dump, the highway that took us there, memory of the gray light that came at sunrise. Those memories seem to come from somewhere. Memories of being in a small French car with two agents and a dead body.

Apparently Avner was near a nervous breakdown. He lost several of his friends. After I told him about all the hippy communes in Woodstock, I think he wanted to live there. I heard he wanted to find himself and lead a normal life. His wife had already moved to the United States. Their mission was almost complete. They had gotten many of the people on Golda's list. I heard that Avner felt that what they were doing was wrong. When they killed a terrorist he would be replaced with someone worse. They would cut off the head of a snake and it would be replaced with two. Avner was still missing his meetings.

The old man, Gideon, had a personality akin to

Merlin the Magician. He could orchestrate a project with his eyes closed. A lot of times when I had a job with them, he would say, "Billy go stand on a corner." I said okay. I never asked why, I just did it. Several hours later when the job was over, I left. I never knew why I stood on that corner. Maybe I was a decoy. I just did what I was told. A lot of the lower level agents did not know why they did what they did. Only the guys who knew were at the top. Gideon and I had so many interesting conversations together. One day he says to me. He was angry the first time we met because I spotted him as an agent right away when I knew he was following me on that bus. I knew I was being watched. I saw him looking at me. I just had the feeling he was an agent. That pissed him off. After all he was head of Mossad and was the best. He did not like it that a nobody leftist, hippy, pothead recognized him. He was one of the greatest spies in the world. I told him his little pad and pencil was a dead giveaway. I said to Gideon who was asking me for advice, if you want to be a top agent you have to think outside the box. When it's time to write down secret information you borrow a pencil from your contact. You get a piece of paper from the trash. Think outside the box. Gideon told me he was going to take my suggestions and present them at Mossad training school. He then went on to tell me that he was naming two Mossad scholarships after me. He was going to advertise where Mossad does its recruiting in Israel that two young people who wanted to be artists could have their art degree funded by spending a few years with the Mossad.

One day at Montmartre I went for a walk to relax. There were a lot of agents there that day. Somebody told me something was going down. There were also a lot of plain clothed Interpol Police. I became an expert on recognizing the different agents. So many people had been following me since I met Avner that day in the Louvre. I had been followed by a few dozen agents in the last three months. They were all there that day. I saw Gideon and he was pacing and smoking cigarettes.

I was going down the steps of Montmartre. Two men approached me- one was Avner and the other was Uzi. I said "Avner, after I met you I have been followed, threatened and robbed." He said "don't worry if you did not do anything you have nothing to worry about." Avner had decided to come in after the time he spent missing meetings. He had been in the states. He had flown in on false passports. I said Montmartre is full of agents and cops. Uzi seemed pissed off.

They kept going up the steps to reach the square. I circled around. I went back up the steps in another place. I went into the square, I was approaching clients. I had my portfolio and charcoal. I was soliciting portraits. I came upon a table. Gideon, Avner and a few people who looked like they played for the NFL were sitting there. I asked each if they would like a portrait. One guy told me he was an artist in Israel. The others declined and looked like they were having a meeting. When I got to Gideon he smiled and said 'Selesnick get out of here." Before I did, he told all of them stories about me in Hebrew; they were all cracking up laughing. When he wanted me to understand, he switched to English saying I was a playboy, that I made big money at Montmartre. I was a secret agent, I sold information,

I was connected and knew Mafia guys and different espionage agents all over the world. One guy got up and offered me a job in Prague. Avner was there and looked very pensive and quiet. The guys were having a party. I went home thinking I have gotten to know some interesting people in Paris.

I was spending a little more time on Rue

Quincompoix. The view was nice from Montmartre but the doorways were fun. Each doorway presenting a different half naked costumed beauty.

They were opening a modern art museum one block over called the George Pompidou Art Museum that looked like an art factory/oil refinery. Centre George Pompidou is a complex in the Beauberg section of Paris in the fourth arrondissement. It's near Les Halles and the Marais. The museum was designed in a style of high tech architecture. It houses a vast public library and a modern art museum which is the largest in Europe. It's named after George Pompidou, the president of France between 1969 and 1974, who decided on its creation. It was officially opened in 1977 by President Valery Giscard d'Estaing. We could see it from my window. I painted it all the time.

The clochards with their pushcarts moved on as the neighborhood became gentrified. Galleries were opening all over. A committed socialist once told me, the neighborhood goes downhill when the upper middle class move in. The working women continued to stay. The streets where they worked were always shifting. The hooker scene always moved around street to street. I was still into my Toulouse Lautrec period. I would wander at night just looking, seeing so many things. Small rough bars which would be the meeting place for rough looking French pimps. I had a life outside of Montmartre and the Mossad.

I mentioned before 'the place where I keep those secret thoughts'. The secrets I keep in this box, deep in my head. Well people handle stress in different ways. When I am traumatized and witness something, it goes into that box. I call it amnesia. I had seen some things I could not deal with. Now I realize there are things in there that I cannot remember. There are triggers.... Loud noises from a car, triggers ... a flashing vision of a shooting.

When I needed money, which was all the time, Montmartre was my only option. On my return Gideon was there. When he saw me he said, I thought I told you to leave town. I said I wanted to work full time for him. By the way Mossad agents only get army pay. You practically work for free. I did not care, I wanted to belong.

Actually in another conversation he made me promise I would go back to the states when I finished my degree. I had recently finished. He asked me what I was doing, I said we moved and gave him the address and my new phone number. Out came the little pad and small pencil.

One day I went to work at Montmartre and my Mossad friends said they had another assignment for me. I was to baby sit and entertain a man named Chuck Barris. I heard he wrote the Dating Game and Gong Show and was also deep in the CIA. The Dating game and the Gong Show were well known American TV shows. The Mossad agent who had given me the job said that he was a strange character.

So I met Chuck and did his portrait. He would not look me in the eyes so it was hard to paint him. He asked me what I was doing in Paris. I told him I came to Paris to get my Masters Degree in art from Goddard College. I worked at Montmartre to make money to support my wife and kid. I ended up getting involved in political assassinations by accident. The Mossad told Chuck I was a player with connections. Chuck asked me why I did it. I told him I did it because of the fact that the Jewish people had endured so much suffering.

He asked me what my nom de guerre was and he was not impressed. He might have mentioned some incidents with prostitutes where he fantasized about doing them. I asked him if he was free for dinner and he said his mood could change when he drank. The Mossad told me that Chuck was a contract guy for the CIA. They told me to be nice to him because he had money and maybe he would buy a painting from me. I found later that Chuck did over thirty contracts for the CIA. A lot of people laughed at the assertions of Chuck's hits. The Mossad took him seriously and so did I. He would fly to Paris for the weekend to do jobs for the CIA and the Mossad.

    I was doing jobs for the Mossad almost every day now. I did them out of love and to have friends. Still none of my other artist friends at Montmartre knew I was a Mossad agent. There were so many celebrities that came to Montmartre. Every artist had their own stories; mine was the Mossad, with other artists it could have been having an affair with some film star.

    The same week I did Chuck's portrait, I met Charlie Chaplin and did his portrait. Charlie always said no one recognizes me in Europe. He was with his wife Oona. She was Eugene O'Neil's daughter. They lived in Switzerland and invited me and my family there for the weekend. I did his portrait in one of the back rooms at Montmartre. He said he recognized my last name because he knew David O. Selznick

    The next day Chuck came back and was wearing army fatigues and army boots with a beret and camouflage shirt. I think the Mossad sent him home to change. He stayed in expensive hotels and ate in fancy restaurants, The Mossad agents lived like poor college students. The next day he was back in Montmartre in the right clothes.

    That day his job was to watch me. He ordered me to stay inside a certain perimeter. He was real mean that day. I don't think he felt watching me was that important. After all, I only fingered somebody; caused his death and now the rest of the PLO squad was out to get me. No big deal, people were dying all around me. I dealt with the artist mafia at Montmartre. I dealt with a French left wing girlfriend who wanted to kill me when I fell asleep after climax.

Chuck did not scare me that much. The next day he brought his wife along. Rumor had it that she did hits too. She might have had a secret pen in her handbag that could kill very quietly in a crowded area such as Montmartre. Killing with poison pens had become the latest rage. A Russian agent killed someone in London that summer using a poison pen. Around the same time poison tips on the end of umbrellas were being used.

I was ordered to stand in a certain place and try to get portrait clients.

She stood next to me while Chuck circled around He looked very worried and said that he was on some kind of Mission. I think one of the rogue Mossad agents told him they would not mind if I disappeared. The Mossad told me a few days before that they could not be responsible for me. She began to badger me about my relationships with prostitutes, how often I went and what did I do with them. She was working herself into lather about my modest almost puritanical peccadillos. I thought she was building up her nerve to do me on the spot with a poison pen. They wanted to see if they could get away with a hit in a crowed area.

Finally, she gave me 100 francs and thanked me for my time and said I was free to go set up anywhere l wanted. She gave me a stern warning to stay out of trouble and be nice to my wife. She made a veiled reference that they were experimenting with some new assassination techniques.

One day when I saw Gideon at Montmartre he says come tomorrow I want you to meet someone. He had said be there at one in the early afternoon. Turns out the guy Gideon wants me to meet was one of the top undercover CIA agents in Europe. Apparently the top spooks in the civilized world had knowledge of Operation Wrath of God. They did not know everything, just enough so Gideon's operation did not come crashing down. The polite, early fortyish man in a rumpled suit looked like he rolled out of a spy novel. He had longish hair with a kind of a beach boy look. Someone who would surf. After introductions were made he asked to see my identification. He looked over my papers and made a comment about how adventurers had to be careful these days He was a stereotypical personality that you would see in a spy movie. He was obviously Ivy League from a family with money just like the British spies. The soft-spoken man was introduced as Gordon. I'm not sure why one spymaster to another was drawing me in. I think that they had some special job for me.

On another day he says he wants me to meet someone else. The guy was in his forty's. He was rough looking from a working class family. Gideon tells me he's a cop but more like the F.B.I. he was from Denmark. Gideon says they were working together. The guy was with Gideon a lot of the times. This guy was named Oscar. Oscar told me he did not like hippies or beatniks or potheads like Gideon. Oscar then said he also lumped student protesters in with that group. We had coffee together on a number of occasions. Then Oscar would come to Montmartre when Gideon was not there. Oscar told me he was part of the European contingent who were hunting and taking revenge on terrorists. Oscar sometimes would bring his younger girlfriend who liked to drink. Oscar would get mad at her for drinking so much. She was French. On one of their visits he paid me to do her portrait. She would have a personality change after one glass of wine. A lot of people would drink while having their portraits done. After all it was Montmartre the playground of the world. Sometimes Oscar would talk down to me like I was a criminal. I said, you drink I smoke hash to relax. In his mind that made me an adversary. Then Gideon tells me he has to go away for a few weeks. He wants me as part of my job to meet with him while he was away. Oscar was not the kind of cop that liked art. He was a real redneck but European. So anyway, I told Oscar besides doing portraits at Montmartre , I drew Biblical statues at the Louvre. So he says bring these drawings to Montmartre and show them to me. So I brought them up in this big portfolio and showed him while we were sitting at one of the many cafes up there. Slowly he started being nicer to me and we became friendlier. We both cheated on our wives'; we had that in common. The day I brought everything up there he actually gave me thirty franks for the effort. Then he says to me that I have homework and I said what. He says I want you to research the meaning of the word Gideon. There was not internet in those days. I went home, asked around and looked at some books. When I went back Oscar asked me if I had done my homework. I said I did. I told him that Gideon was a prophet from the Book of Judges. He was a judge of the Israelites who became famous when he led a battle with three hundred men against a much larger force. Gideon then would punish people who turned to worshipping idols. Gideon was known on taking revenge with a vengeance. Oscar was trying to tell me something. I suppose my friend Gideon told Oscar I needed some education. I was so out of my league that I just kept going and acted cavalier about my involvement. Cops in Europe did not have a lot of dough. They made what American cops made.

Memoirs of an Artist

When Gideon came up to Montmartre, and I was not there, he would talk to artists and ask questions about me and tell the other artists that he was investigating me for a drug gang connection.

These girls from Trenton were visiting who had connections to a drug ring. They had taken some of my art home with them and were going to try to sell them for me. One was called a Van Dyke after the famous artist who hung in the Louvre. I called my friend in Trenton a few days later and I said did you sell the Van Dyke. She sounded annoyed and said sounds like this phone is tapped and hung up. The girl I called in Trenton was a childhood friend who became a wise guy drug dealer in her teens. She was in a family owned vending machine business. Her name was Sammie and lived in New Jersey but worked for a Mobster in Boston organized crime.

The next day Gideon said to me. Did you sell the Van Dyke? I said you know she really is trying to sell my art. Do I care that she sells Thai sticks. Gideon had my phone tapped. Sammie had a friend, also from Trenton, as her partner, who went by the name Nicky. Her father was named "Swiss Cheese" because he put holes in people. They operated a Bakery/Deli in the Little Italy section of Trenton called Chambersburg.

He had gotten his start driving for Bugsy Siegel. That was before Bugsy moved to Hollywood. Swiss Cheese was a ladies man like his boss Bugsy. Swiss Cheese had been married three times and had his daughter Nicki with his third wife.

Nicki and Sammie were what was known as Lipstick Lesbians. They were both very hot and attracted a lot of attention from men. They would do threesomes with men who wanted to have sex with two women at the same time. This was expensive because they were both very attractive. Nicki had short hair in a very stylish cut. She was five foot eight and a half, a lean one hundred and 10 pounds, and her forte was roaming the rooftops of Paris by the light of the moon. Sammie had perfect manners and would give you the shirt off her back and was a big spender. Sammie was five foot ten inches slender with long blond curly hair. She had bee stung lips and was a real knock out. Sammie and Nick were just big pot and hash dealers from around my home town. They would do threesomes with men when they were on the road. They usually met these men in airports. They both dressed to the nines. They would wear expensive black leather outfits with spike heels. They started out selling weed in nightclubs in New Jersey and Philadelphia. They then graduated to selling weight around the east coast.

Sammie and Nicky were part of an international drug gang. They were buying Thai sticks in Thailand and bringing them to the states to sell. Paris was the staging ground for the Thai stick operation. A Thai stick is a 6-inch stick with marijuana, grown in Thailand wrapped around it. It was considered very exotic. They worked for a man who ran the operation. All I can say about Sammie and Nicki's boss was that his nickname was "Chairman of the Board." He traveled with just one bodyguard. His bodyguard also was his driver and valet. They were both traveling on a Mexican passport. They were arriving in a few weeks and would be staying at the Crillion Hotel. That joint was long known as a meeting place for spies and intrigue. During World War two it was headquarters for the Gestapo. Gideon knew about my clandestine meeting at the Crillion.

The Chairman of the Board did buy a lot of art from me over the years. For that, I am very grateful. He came from a rich socially and politically connected family in

Mexico. He had a lot of international businesses and he did weed and hash on the side. He also did a lot of cocaine and was always partying with beautiful women.

Basically I hated hanging around with the Chairman but I needed him. He would come over and want to do coke. At this point I realized cocaine was not for me. The only thing I liked about coke was that you could make love for twenty- four hours straight. He would buy a piece of art every hour or so. I really wanted him to leave but he would keep buying work so he could stay. Basically he was paying me to do coke with him. He also took Cindy and me to a lot of expensive restaurants in Paris.

I tried to keep my relationship with the Chairman separate from my relationship with Gideon. They both knew about each other. The Chairmen also loved Israel and the Jewish people. The Chairmen was Catholic and had been to Israel to visit the Cristian holy sites.

At night when Cindy was asleep the Chairman and I would walk around my neighborhood.

It was in the summer. I would talk about Toulouse and check out the doorways. The Chairmen loved whores. What doorway are we going in now, he would ask. Each doorway a different uniform, a different fantasy. It was like the novel Steppenwolf by Herman Hesse.

Another thing we did in Paris in warm weather was to go to the pool. It was called the Pisine Deliney. It was a pool in a huge barge that was moored in the River Seine right outside the Quartier Latin in, the left bank on the river. It was a totally French experience. You would pay an entrance fee to get in. There were small cabanas that you would rent to change in and you would have these cabanas all day. Many people went to these cabanas for changing and to have quickie sex French style. Everything about going to the pool was attitude. Everyone was practically naked so all you had was your face, your body and your attitude - the way you looked at people and the way they looked at you. Many words could be spoken in just a glance, and that was what the pool was all about. It was getting the right kind of looks from people and ending up in the cabanas.

I liked Gideon and spent a lot of time with him at Montmartre. I was always trying to convince him that I was not a sleaze ball. I was a serious artist and not dangerous. He was always saying I knew things that were harmful to the state of Israel. I knew they were all spies but did not know they were the "superstars." Even though I did jobs for the Mossad, I was occasionally still treated like the enemy. That's because I smoked pot and hash and harbored left wing views.

I told Gideon about my problems with amnesia; we talked about it a lot. There were things I could not remember that had to do with violence and death. When I fingered that PLO bad guy and caused his demise, it almost did not register with me. I wanted to be accepted so badly by the Israelis. I was glad to be of help. I rarely thought about it afterward. The fact that they were ultra right wingers did not bother me. They did not hate blacks. They thought women should have a right to choose. They were right wing on Arab militants.

Now writing about it, more details are coming back. The day the PLO hash dealer, assassin disappeared, when I was told to go home after, I saw his young accomplices with worried looks on their faces. Where was their leader? The look of worry is universal. Yes, they were the bad guys, but yes, their faces displayed the same look as the Israelis when they lost one of their own. After the agents took Big Daddy away, I was told to go home but to take a specific route to the subway. When I did I saw Steve at the subway who also told me to go home and be careful. I was in danger. I really was not too scared. It was all so unbelievable that I could not fully understand what was happening. He said he would look after me in the sense that he would chase down Big Daddy's teenage entourage. He implied that the accomplices might come to find me and take revenge. He had his bomber jacket on. The coat was opened and there was a pistol in his belt. It looked like an old gun from World War Two. I later learned that Steve chased the teenagers out of town. They were driving their hotrod and Steve was in pursuit with his old car. When he got close and pulled up along- side of them he waved his piece. The teenagers had relatives in the south of France and that's where they were heading. From there they slipped back in to Hebron in the West Bank.

 I still would return to Montmartre to work doing portraits. One day, when I was having another incredible conversation with Gideon, I blurted out something about Israel being the fifty third state. Gideon almost had a conniption. This had rankled him. He says Israel was grateful for all its help from America. He said that he and his friends in the military felt if necessary Israel could make it on its own. He got emotional about it. I said okay. It was just an expression that I had heard. I would not bring it up again.

 As usual I needed money. The portrait hustle grew tiring. I had a friend named Pascal. He was from Paris. He was short and skinny with an elf like face. He looked like Peter Pan but with dark hair and eyes. He hung at Montmartre, but he was an errand boy for some French gamblers from some of the back rooms. He had most of his upper teeth but was missing the ones on the side. He was quiet, but always had a grin on his face. He had a childlike nature. His claim to fame was when he was fourteen he fucked a ninety-year-old woman and got a five-dollar tip.

When I hung with him, we would smoke hash and he would obsessively sharpen his bowie knife on a pumice stone. He was a wannabe merc, eager to make his bones and move up. A lot of mercenaries had been hanging out at Montmartre. They liked to party there. Some of them were Americans who were body guards for the rich and famous. Pascal did errands for the French mob. There was intermingling between mercs and the mob.

We knew a lot of artists that were looking for hash and we thought we could make a few bucks. I was the one with the great connection in the souk. My PLO terrorist friends had split town, one by way of the dump, and the teenagers headed south in their hot rods. We were planning a nighttime run to the souk in the "east Jerusalem" section of Paris. I was armed with my day's pay hustling portraits. Pascal had his knife under his pant leg in a leather leg sheaf and his new set of dentures. We took the Metro to Barbes Rochechouart and proceeded on foot to Belleville. The colorful Africans in their native garbs crowded the streets. Games of Three Cards Monte were played on cardboard boxes on the sidewalks. All this was going on under the raised metro platform. African women were walking the streets selling their wares, which included sex.

The smells of outdoor cooking and herb and spice markets permeated the air. Le Flic was rounding up the dealers with the Three Cards Monte games, mostly North African and Africans. Few French ventured into this part of town. The ones that did would come for the inexpensive department store called Tati. We walked towards our destination and the streets grew quieter. We came closer to the winding alleys of Belleville which were dark and foreboding.

We spotted an Arab looking teenager in a large doorway. It wasn't a doorway into a house it was more like a doorway into a courtyard. I was a known artist even there. I had been to that area frequently to make buys. We entered the doorway and approached the teenage hash dealer and I removed some one hundred franc bills from my pocket and made the transaction. Usually the teenagers run in pairs, his friend came out the door. He had been taking a dump in one of those holes they called bathrooms. The second teenager greeted us and we left.

As we were leaving the area two figures jumped out of the shadows with knifes in their hands and demanded our money and fingers of hashish. It was the two teenagers we were with in the courtyard. They had followed us out and decided to rob us. Pascal quickly drew his knife hidden in a sheaf tied around his lower leg under his pants. He swung the knife across the chest of one of the attackers. The teenager fell to the ground. His friend ignored us and tended to his fallen comrade. It was happening in slow motion. We then took off running as if we were doing a fifty-yard dash.

We made it to the Boulevard, crossed over and grabbed a cab. I did not want another murder on my conscience; my plan was to make a buy and turn it for a profit up on Montmartre. I knew that the hash came from the Bekka Valley in Lebanon and the money made in Paris funded the killing of Jews.

The cab took us to our destination which was Saint Germaine des Prey. First stop was the all night pharmacy for some French Robotussin to ease the pain and catch a buzz. Then we went to a famous all night place called the English pub. This English pub was multi-leveled and open all night. It was a gathering place for French hippies, North African drug dealers, French drug dealers and users, and wannabe terrorist vampires and French insomniacs.

To get in you knock on this old wooden door. Then a small window opens, which hinges on the side like a small door, and some guy from the inside checks you out. Then he closes the little window and they let you in. Metal detectors were not in use yet.

That place was like the French version of the Fillmore East in the east village of New York City. First you step in and go down a few steps. There was a long bar. It felt sunken. The room was filled with all kinds of smoke, different smells- Pipe tobacco, French Galloise cigarettes, grass, and hash, opium. It was a smoke filled haze. There were booths on the side filled with teenagers, students, tourists, and hippies. Some of the tables looked like they were French hoods or drug dealers. We all knew one another.

At the end of the first floor, there were steps that took you to these different dining rooms with booths. This was an all night hangout. We moved a few fingers to different tables of French hippies. We settled on a booth next to a group of young women. They soon joined us. One was fat to obese, and in France after midnight, a luxury item. Pascal was in love. Mine was short with very full, very red lips, medium bosom and six-inch spikes on her heels.

Later that night, Pascal and I were walking home. All the Hash in the world could not compensate the fear and anxiety that swept over me. Maybe those teenagers worked indirectly worked for Abu Nidal. They drew first blood by attacking us. In twenty-four hours we sold most of the hash, keeping a supply for ourselves. I did not do the actual stabbing and did not want to but we were defending ourselves. It's easy to forget incidents like that. That box in the bottom right hand side of my brain was becoming a larger storage unit. When Big Daddy disappeared I forgot about it. However, when I was with Pascal and we had that incident with the teenager, my memories of big daddy came back.

At nights when I stayed home and was not drawing I would read. My passion for studying the Holy Books brought me to a place where I reexamined pagan cults. I was a committed Jew but wanted to understand all things. I concluded that the pagan religions of Israel evolved into the Wicca religion.

In between my experiences at Montmartre with the Mossad, I would relax at the nude figure class at the Ecole des Beaux art. As I recounted before there was always screaming matches between students and teachers. That was entertaining in its self. It would be interesting to see who capitulated first. I had never seen that at American classes. I think it was nonexistent. The teacher was a youngish woman with short reddish blond hair. A revolutionary herself and a recent graduate, she was forced to respond in kind to the agitated revolutionary student. As I recall he was a faux Che type beret and red scarf to boot. Also a lot of perverts would sit in as non- inscribed students. They wanted the chance to gawk at a nude free of charge. I was a non inscribed student. That class was really a trip.

There was another course where I asked to sit in. It was about Old Master techniques. You learned to paint with egg tempera paint. You could grind your own colors. The teacher was a man named Abraham. He was from Jerusalem. He was the son of a Rabbi who taught Kabbala. He was a bearded sage and he said I could join the class. He showed me pictures of his paintings. They were surreal painting of biblical scenes. Colorful drug induced hallucinations of biblical visions. His classes were like going to religious services. I became his student and a series of events unfolded.

Kabala, also spelled Cabala, is an esoteric method and discipline, a school of thought. It is a book which is the secret teaching of the Old Testament. There are different theories as to its origins. Some purport that the Cabala is as old as the Old Testament itself. It was first recognized by scholars in 1100. One theory tells that it was written by one man named Moses de Lyon. Moses de Lyon was from Lyon, France. Mainstream Judaism does not even accept Cabala as a legitimate book in Jewish philosophy. There was a town in Israel called Safed. It was in the north in the mountains. Later I visited there. The philosophy of Cabala originated there. There were schools of Rabbis that taught it there. And that's ongoing presently.

Abraham, besides being a sage and a super artist, sat at the feet of a Hindu yogi from India. He had two friends who sponsored him. After becoming Abraham's student, I was invited to a lecture and demonstration at a private apartment in Paris. I arrived at the designated hour and met a holy man from India. He was wearing a sari and sandals. He had hair down to his spine and had an intelligent serious face. I sat in for a lecture.

Then this Hindu sage practiced healing techniques on people. Abraham had told me some stories about him. He came from the jungles in southern India. He came from a lineage of Hindu teachers. They practiced and were masters of yoga. They had taken their vows of poverty and shunned technology and embraced nature. One of the tricks he could do was to put a watering hose in his mouth, let the water flow continually, and have the water flush out through his penis simultaneously. I went to several of their meetings and more incidents were to follow.

I had a thing for museums. I did a lot of work in the Louvre. I met Avner there. Well I had been to other museums too and had love affairs with some of them. Paris is not only the art capital of the world but it is the museum capital as well. My favorites were the small ones tucked away in hard to get to places. One of my favorite artists was Gustav Moreau. He was in my top ten artist list. He had a small, intimate museum in Paris.

He was born 1826 and lived to 1898 he was a French Symbolist painter whose paintings were of biblical and mythological figures. I considered him in the same school of Fuchs. Moreau was also popular with symbolist writers. He was known for his eccentric personality. In his lifetime he produced over eight thousand paintings. The Gustav Moreau Museum is his former workshop and opened in 1903. Andre Breton used to hang out there and regarded Moreau as the father of Surrealism. I discovered this little known museum and made many pilgrimages there as well. The place was so cool. It really was indescribable. He used to live there as well. It's in a beautiful neighborhood of large mansions. There are three or four floors which are open to the public. His works are left as if Gustav Moreau was still there. Often I would go there alone and be the only visitor in the place. I would experience what I would describe as accelerated learning, religious experiences. I would leave feeling so drained yet so fulfilled. I was there in his workshop. My God, his output was unbelievable!

My other Museum experience which had a religious like effect on me was called the Guimet Museum. That is the museum of Asian Art in the sixteenth arrondissement in Paris. It is one of the largest collection of Asian art outside of Asia. It was founded in 1889 by Emille Guimet, a French industrialist who traveled there extensively. I was just an uneducated boy from Trenton who was now getting exposed to this incredible art. After going there at night I would have these strange dreams about the place.

The Jeu de Paume Museum, which housed the Impressionists, was another place to make what I call a sacred pilgrimage. Originally it was built as a tennis court for French nobility in the seventeenth century. It was located in the Tuilleries Garden. During the French Revolution it was a hang-out for the Revolutionary forces. During the German Occupation in World War Two, it was used as a storage facility for art stolen from other museums and from Jewish collections. Art Shows were staged for high ranking German officers. After the war the museum was rededicated as a museum for impressionists and post impressionists. O M G That stands for oh my God, that was how I felt after the first time I went there. What an education!

I had finished my degree with Goddard College. I was not going to get my small family stipend any more. My father said, time to get off the tit. My father was waiting for me to finish my degree so he could discontinue a small monthly amount of money he was giving me so I could work on my degree.

Montmartre was too stressful with the Mossad there watching my every move, and people like Chuck Barris practicing assassination techniques on me. Also the artist Mafia (Pierre) was always threatening to beat me up for working there.

I was always looking for ways to make money so I could do my art. I tried to have a show in a coffee house at lle Sainte Louis near Notre Dame. An American friend that I had met at the Beaux Arts had introduced me to the owner. The proprietor spoke no English and very fast impatient French. He said yes to the show and I thought he said okay for the Fiche, a big poster. I spent a fortune on it. It was a big self portrait of me in Bas-relief and wings. I called it the lost Bas-relief of King Solomon's temple.

When I showed the owner of the cafe he got really mad. He acted like it was too weird and had the name Solomon's temple in it. He's thought it was political rather than mystical. He thought the title would attract a terrorist bomb. I was very naïve. After all bombs were going off almost every week in Paris at that time. Other artists could paint Old Testament themes. I got mad and tried reporting him to the American embassy.

Around the time I left Paris I got very famous in the city of light. A famous French newspaper, I think it was le Monde, did a story about the poster being frowned on by the owner of the coffee shop. The article talked about cynicism in French culture, and an attitude of gloom. I was referred to as a light or shining star. The article said something like, "despite all of the bombings in the city, people need the positive energy of art." Gideon told me this in a telephone call months later.

I finally had had enough of Paris and being broke. I heard you could get tickets home from the American Embassy. The American Embassy is the oldest United States diplomatic mission. Benjamin Franklin and some of the founding fathers were the earliest ambassadors to France. It is located on two avenues, Gabriel and the North West corner of Place de Concorde in the eighth arrondissement. It is something to stand near there and see this famous Egyptian Obelisk standing in the middle of Place de Concorde. Also the Hotel Crillion is right around the corner. I think the famous restaurant Maxims is next door to the Crillion. I knew a lady there. I met her when I reported the guy that did not like my poster for the art show. She liked my art and she visited me at my gallery in the states several years later.

Going to the American Embassy is an adventure, especially in Paris. Marines stand guard outside the embassy. You go through a little booth where there is a metal detector. Inside there is a level of attitude that is comforting.

When you tried to get free tickets home to the states, they would call your parents first and pressure them to pay for your tickets home. We prepped Cindy's mother in advance. We told Bunny, Cindy's mother, to plead poverty. I told them I was estranged from my parents. They were pressuring me for names and numbers. They finally found out my parents had a villa in the south of France. When they were about to call, I left. I went to my father's office in Mount Rouge, I told the secretary that my father said it was okay for a set of tickets. They gave them to me.

The American Express office is located at 11 Rue de Scribe. It has been serving tourists since the 1900's when its opening coincided with the Paris Exposition. The American Express office is a place that's another freak show, especially if you go there every month to pick up your monthly check. If I remember correctly, it's near the famed opera house where Marc Chagall did the murals on the ceiling. The characters there are out of a Thomas Wolfe novel.

A month before we left, I made a phone call to my parents. I called even though we were estranged. My father said some mysterious man approached him at his golf club in the south of France. The man introduced himself to my father and said, "your son Billy has some undesirable friends."

I told this American guy who was to be a soldier of fortune, that I was leaving my apartment. I knew him from a busker bar. Buskers are musicians, usually British, who sang at movie ques. That's a line of people waiting to get into a movie. Cindy and I would go with them and let our young son collect. That was done with a hat and costume. The busker bar was where the buskers counted their money and drank beer and did bottles of cough medicine. It was one of my hangouts when we were in the left bank.

This rough character named Rudi claimed to have a metal plate in his head. That was from a job he did in the Congo. He operated out of Belgium but liked Paris. He had been in Vietnam. He originally was from the Rio Grande valley in south Texas, along the border with Mexico. He left there because he was involved in a murder and he had to leave town. We wanted to let him take over our apartment. He had nothing to do with the Mossad. I have cool friends all over town. I knew mercenaries everywhere. They were in the Left Bank, they were at Montmartre. He moved in and we moved out and flew home. The landlord lived in Neims and we wired him the money on the first. We told our friend to do it and showed him how at the bank. After we left, he tried to wire money, or he was late. There was a mix up. The landlord got mad and wanted him out.

I think after we left town Gideon was there. He told this guy that they were interested in me. Gideon may have helped him out and rented the apartment himself for young Mossad agents on scholarships. I heard that he got in touch with the landlord and introduced himself as a police officer from Interpol. He told the landlords the apartment would be used once in a while. I was not fully aware of it at time but Operation Wrath of God was winding down.

Avner had come in and then immigrated to the states. Steve returned to Israel and received a high position in security for the state of Israel. Gideon eventually retired.

I accomplished some things during my trip to Paris between 1974 and 1977. I finished my Masters degree with Goddard College. I was exposed to French culture. I worked at the Louvre doing copies. I worked doing portraits at Montmartre. I made friends with artists from all over the world. I sat in on classes at the Ecole Des Beaux Art. I learned about Trompe L'oeil. I was exposed to and learned to love classical architecture. I ate fine French foods. I made love to French women. And I also became a spy and got to know the top spies from that era. Not only did I become a spy, but a well- known one at that. After I got home my character began to appear in certain books and movies. Things did not end after arriving in the states.

The three terrorist leaders that Avner's team did not find were Ali Hassan Salameh, Abu Daoud and Dr. Waddi Hadad. Hadad died of natural causes in 1978 in an East German hospital. ln 1981, Abu Dauod was shot in the lobby of a hotel in Poland, but he was not killed. On January 22, 1979, Salameh, and several of his bodyguards, were blown up when his Chevrolet station wagon passed a parked Volkswagen near the corner of rue Verdun and

Madame Curie in Beirut.

Chapter Four

I arrived at JFK with my family, penniless. Custom agents found two 300-year-old skulls that I got in the catacombs in Paris, in our luggage. I told them I drew them. It was true. They let me go. Here's what happened. We got in line to go through customs. It was me, my wife, and my son. We had several suitcases and I had a half-a-dozen portfolios. Wherever I went I was harassed because of my appearance. Our time came and we approached the customs agent. He started opening all our suitcases. He had not yet got to the suitcase that had the skulls. I knew he was going to open that bag. I decided to start prepping him in advance saying, I was an artist and that I did drawings of skulls. He seemed uninterested. He came to the suitcase with the skulls in them. He said "what's this?" and pulled out a 300- year- old skull. And again, I said that I drew them. He shook his head in disbelief and decided just to let us go through. He even let me keep the skulls. They looked at all my art too.

When we finally got through customs, who did I see but my mother. One hour earlier she had dropped my father off for a flight back to Europe. My mother gave us a ride to Cindy's mother's place.

She informed us on the way there that they had just bought a farm in Newtown. My mother said that she wanted us to stay at Cindy's mother's because my sister was staying at the farm, and there was no room for us. (Even though it had seven bedrooms and sixteen fireplaces in the main house.)

It had four one-bedroom apartments in another building. There was also a huge barn and a few other buildings. Another guy was staying there named Peter.

He was going to be the caretaker. And my sister and her family were going to watch the farm.

It's called sibling rivalry. Our feelings were very hurt. They thought I was overbearing and too eccentric. Oh well.

I arranged a show at the Jewish community center in Trenton, New Jersey. It was in January of 1977. I had a big opening and many people I knew came. It was well attended and I sold a lot of pieces.

I played the "eccentric" role to a tee. I purchased a three-piece suit at an expensive men's clothing store. I had not slept for two nights before my show and I was near a manic state. I had traded some art for some coke. I sold the coke to pay for the frames. I also used the cocaine to share with my friends and clients in Trenton.

I was a local celebrity. I got a big write-up from the Trenton Times and a few other newspapers and magazines. Many doctors were buying my work. Many old friends were coming out of the woodwork. I was starting to be noticed.

I sent a copy of my write-up to Gideon; I addressed it to the Mossad office in Paris. I heard he got it and was showing it to artists at Montmartre. I was so bizarre, that I got several write-ups in newspapers. Then several magazine articles came about me. I began to develop a knack for getting publicity for my work. I was getting scores of write-ups. I think I was doing it to keep a shell of writers around myself. It had something to do with what the Mossad was doing to me. Following me everywhere. The newspaper articles gave me a sense of protection. In a way, I see it now as beating them at their own game.

I also was selling work to these female drug dealers. It was fun to hang out with them. They had money and liked to have fun. They were always paying for hookers and treating in expensive restaurants. The high end hookers were from Manhattan and they would get them for their male friends as presents. I was hanging with my friend Sammie, from an Organized Crime Family in Boston, and Nickie whose father was in the deli/bakery business. Sammie, the girl with the mob connections, was a girl I knew from high school. Her friend and bodyguard, Nickie was also an acquaintance from high school. My father knew her father because they were both businessmen in Trenton. Sammie and Nickie were basically high level pot dealers that did a lot of cocaine for fun. Sammie had a pet parrot that would talk. I did a painting of it. They bought a lot of paintings from me. Their friends also bought a lot of work from me. I really appreciate that.

Anyway, when Sammy and Nicky were in Paris, Sammy said that he was going to act as my agent and help me sell my work. So, when I got back to the states Sammy and Nicky were the first people I looked up.

After my opening, I sold some pieces and got ready to move back to Woodstock, where the

Mossad came to see me.

At the time, I had been experimenting with snorting cocaine. I was trading paintings for it. I liked it at first, and snorted it for about a year on weekends. It was just as great of a sexual stimulant as the LSD. I was getting the cocaine from Sammy.

After a year I slowed down and finally quit. At first I enjoyed it. You could have sex for hours. Then I grew intolerant to it. I needed more and more all the time. It made me too tense. There are also side effects of paranoia. I never did it every day. It was a weekend kind of thing.

My world still went by what was going on in the Middle East. It was still an obsession. Egypt and Israel signed a peace treaty in 1979. It was signed in Oslo by

Menachem Begin and Anwar Sadat. They were both awarded the Nobel Peace Prize.

Anwar Sadat came to Jerusalem and spoke at the Knesset. In 1981 Anwar Sadat was assassinated by some fundamentalist army officers. The world mourned. Only the good die young.

SELF PORTRAIT ON MAPLE LANE

We rented a log cabin in Woodstock on Maple Lane, where it met Tannery Brook Road. That was in the center of town. Town was a hamlet of about two thousand people. Half the businesses were art galleries. There were several restaurants and assorted other shops. Cindy got a job in a dress shop. Joshua was in school.

On New Year's eve I got a phone call late in the evening and the man calling was drunk and sounded like he was crying. He said he was a guy that I knew in Paris. One of the Israeli team was an American. He was a marine in Vietnam and saw a lot of action including hand to hand combat and when he got out went to work for the Israelis. We spent a lot of time talking at Montmartre. He worked for Gideon. He said he drank a lot especially on New Year's. New Year's Eve was the only night that Gideon would take his calls. He needed people to talk to. At the time the stuff I did was so deep in my box that I had a hard time having a conversation with him. He said that "the powers that be" in Israel considered him unstable and he could not visit any more.

PENCIL DRAWING

I got a show at a good gallery called The Ann Leonard gallery. Ann Leonard was a French speaking lady from Antwerp. She was Jewish and her family had died in the concentration camps. She came to the states in the 1950's and moved to Woodstock. She met a man named Bruce Leonard. They started dating and eventually got married. Bruce turned out to have mental problems and they got divorced. She kept his last name.

I got some more write ups and made a few sales. Cindy liked her job but I was restless in Woodstock. We began to fight about it. I would still fool around but I would be very discreet about it.

Woodstock, by then, had had its heyday. It was not as crowded as it was around the time of the festival of 1969.

This guy named Marty owned a deli in town. His good looking wife Sharon used to work there too. He was involved in a big drug bust. These young Mossad agents, who were in Woodstock, asked him to try to get information from me. It seemed Avner had disappeared again and the Mossad wanted him back. The agents intimated that maybe it could help Marty at his sentencing. They had connections with federal judges. Marty was willing but wanted to record it. There were a lot of musicians in town who had "hidden" mikes. He invited me to a get together on top of his deli, to secretly record me. I told him about my time in Paris and what I was doing. I even brought my portfolio with me with some original art.

After he "questioned" me, he showed me a magazine from some hippy publication (I think it was called Mother Earth). He told me he wanted me to read an article in it. I read the article from this hippy alternative magazine. It was Avner's story. The Mossad was after him. He wanted to hide or drop out or retire. I think the article said that Avner moved to a commune and Avner dropped acid with them. He wanted to become a citizen of the U.SA. It even had the part about the hit squad, but it did not register with me. It was like a dream.

Marty asked me what I thought of the article and if I knew him. I lied and said it sounds familiar. I met a lot of interesting people in Paris. He then started to badger me about my association with the Mossad. He said the Mossad was not interested in me because I did studies on the near east. I said Israel craves social contacts because of their isolation at the UN. Marty started pressuring me for information and I said I did not know. Finally, I asked him about his bust and he got pissed. My opinion on Marty was that he was a selfish drug dealer, a weasel trying to get his sentence lowered. He went around town saying I was sleazy. I think he sold large quantities of heroin and opium, either from Afghanistan or the Golden Triangle. That also funded terrorism and the killing of Jews.

When I left the deli someone told me that he was secretly recording me.

I was a Jew with emotional ties to Israel and an artist pothead. Despite the fact that the Mossad was using me, I would do it over the same way if I had the chance. The Mossad was looking for Avner. They thought I could help them because I told Avner about hippy communes when I talked to him in the Louvre in Paris. Avner did not want to be found.

I went to Joshua's café. Joshua was an Israeli who looked like a Mossad agent. He owned an Israeli restaurant in the center of town. Some other guys were standing with him, clean-cut football player types. They also looked like Mossad agents. They had been hanging out there. I said to Joshua, "what does the Mossad want from me."

The "clean cut football players" asked me if I wanted to talk to the old man, Gideon. I gave them my number and went home, and he called.

He asked me how Cindy and I were doing. Finally, he said I was his only lead to Avner. Avner wanted to stay in the states. I didn't know if they knew where he was. The article said he was in a commune near Boston. Gideon asked me to go there and look for him. I told him I did not have a car. I told Gideon that I thought my civil rights were being violated.

While this was happening, some people in town

were saying I was responsible for killing women and children in a terrorist incident; that I was for the side of the PLO killing Jews. This happened when I was in Paris. How absurd. I helped the Mossad get a PLO drug guy. I had been shot at. I saw a few people die near me. Those were comments made from misunderstood info when those Mossad agents were asking around about me behind my back. They said they wanted information about me because I was involved in some espionage and terrorism. They said I was a drug user, therefore nefarious and had information concerning secrets about the state of Israel. The secrets – that I had met Avner, penetrated the security wall, met the old man and got in over my head. I told Gideon then that people in town were accusing me of being a PLO terrorist. He said that was ridiculous and he tried to straighten it out around town.

Then Gideon told me about this newspaper article, and I was famous in Paris. There was an article in Le Monde, a famous newspaper in Paris. It spoke of an artist who made a giant poster of a painting depicting himself as a winged griffin. The proprietor of the café where the art show was being held had an objection to the word King Solomon. He was afraid it would attract negative attention to his establishment. After all, there were bombs going off every few days.

Paris then was like Beirut. Many bombs were targeting anything Jewish. My vision was truly of a mystical sacred place, having no idea of its political implications. There were references to the proprietor, that his name had Arab sounding roots. The article stated that it was "refreshing in an age of cynicism that an artist had to suffer the consequences of a jaded and cynical society." That I was "like a shining light in a dark universe."

When the Mossad came to town people talked

because they were asking a lot of questions about me. Avner and Steve and the rest of the boys were super heroes. Gideon had no other leads and considered me a threat to the state of Israel because I had embarrassing information. They did not want any newspaper stories about Israel that were embarrassing.

Sometimes I felt like Public Enemy number one. Gideon and I finished our conversation; he sounded like he was around the corner.

I continued with my obsession with studying mystical literature. Woodstock was the perfect place for it. There were many extremists in town and there were a lot of religious cults around the town. So it was a place I could feel comfortable. I had gone in my studies from pure Torah student to being lead down the path of paganism to Wicca. My readings were now centered on understanding the Old Testament from a secular scholarly point of view, free of religious interference. I could read the Old Testament now and know what period of biblical history my passage came from. I knew what the idols looked like that Israel's foes were worshipping. I knew what biblical people looked like from studying their iconography.

My readings took me closer to the time period of Masada, a Jewish revolt and the Essenes. They were members of an ascetic sect that existed in ancient Palestine from the second century B.C. to the third century A.D.

The Essenes were a group that seceded from Zadokite priests and were less in number than the Pharisees and the Sadducees, the two other major sects of the times. The Essenes lived in various cities. They had a communal life. It was dedicated to asceticism, poverty, daily immersions in water and abstinence from worldly pleasure, including some who practiced celibacy. Many separate but related groups of that era shared similar mystic beliefs.

The Essenes have gained fame in modern times as the result of a discovery known as the Dead Sea Scrolls. These were a large group of religious documents which were the Essenes library. The documents include multiple copies of the Hebrew bible untouched from as early as three hundred B.C. They immersed themselves in water every morning, ate together after prayer, devoted themselves to charity and benevolence, forbade the expression of anger, studied the holy books and protected their secrets. And they were mindful of the names of angels kept in their secret writings.

The Essenes would have fit right in around Woodstock. There were already groups like them scattered around the mountains in the Catskills. Many of these groups and cults had taken over some old hotels in the area. The Catskills were known for being an inexpensive vacation area for Jews who lived in New York City. The resorts and hotels that catered to these people had gone out of business and many religious groups were taking them over.

My wife and I had a strange encounter with one such group. They were more like a cult. There was a protestant church in the center of Woodstock on the village green. On Friday nights the church let these members of a religious cult use their facilities. On Friday night, members of this group would walk around Woodstock and talk to various people, mostly hippies and flower children. That's when Cindy and I met them. We were walking around town one and we were approached by two clean cut looking men. They told us they were ex- hippies from California and they wanted to share something with us. They said they were part of the U.F.O. movement there. They had several sightings and encounters and that led them to something better. They said they used to have long hair, dressed in robes, and were very adept in yoga. Then they had a transformation. They wanted to talk further about it and we invited them to our house. There the conversation continued, and they told us that they found God through Jesus. I thought how boring and mainstream. They lived in this religious commune in the Catskills, in an old hotel, and came to Woodstock on Friday nights. We continued to talk and they left us with some books and said they would be back next Friday night.

The next weekend they returned. They got me away from my wife. They got me to agree to meet them in the church in the center of town. They took me into the sanctuary and both started to pray. I was standing, watching them. They prayed so hard that they put themselves into a trance. Their eyes were shut. They became enveloped in a golden light. I felt strange. The next thing I knew they were speaking in some strange language. They told me later they were speaking in tongues. That was the language of the angels and it was both eternal and from ancient times. Neither spoke this language previously; it only happened when possessed by the Holy Spirit. I felt stranger and stranger. Then this feeling came over me. I felt the invisible spirit of a being who told me that he was the spirit of Jesus Christ. This spirit was trying to force its way into me and get me to fall down on the floor and yell, I love Jesus Christ. I felt I liked being Jewish, and if I fell to the floor that would be the end of my Jewishness. Besides I did not want to get a haircut and look like them. I did not want to stop having oral sex with chubby chicks. I fought this urge. It was the roughest fight I ever had. This spirit was real and it was trying to knock me down to the floor. My friends by now were withering like snakes, eyes closed, strange tongues like a song, so spiritual so perfect. It was way more out there than acid. The session finally closed down and they regained their composure and switched back to English. They thought it a shame that I never let the Holy Spirit in. They left some more books and I never saw them again. The speaking of tongues is the fluid vocabulary or unconscious flow of speech-like syllables that lack any readily comprehensive meaning. In some cases, it's part of a religious practice. Some people consider it a sacred language. It's most commonly practiced in Pentecostal and Charismatic Christianity, but it is also practiced by non-Christians. Glossolalle speech does resemble human language, according to a linguist from University of Toronto.

One day, this attractive woman approached me on the village green in Woodstock. She told me she was pissed at this Mossad agent who seduced her and wanted her to find out information about me. She said that they had had sex under false pretenses. She told me that my civil rights had been violated and I should go to the papers. I said I wanted all of it to go away. I told her I was going to ignore it until I couldn't.

She said she wanted to write a book about it. She tried to talk me into selling my story to some publication in Greenwich Village. I basically pushed all this information into a box that was buried very deep in my brain. Looking back, I am glad I did. How would it have been for the rest of my life seeing the world through the lens of the war between Israel and the P.L.O. I did not want to be famous for being a Mossad groupie. I wanted to be famous for my art.

I never ratted on the rogue Mossad, though, I was too scared for that. I never sold information to hurt the state of Israel, I was too Jewish for that.

One morning I woke up and went outside my house, and who did I see standing at the end of my street but Gideon. I thought I was tripping. I said what you are doing here. He said shut up, this is important. He smashed a cigarette between his fingers and threw it to the ground. He acted as if he did not want to be there. He said Avner had run out on the Mossad and wanted to stay in the States, and that he was coming to Woodstock today to talk to me because I was his responsibility. Gideon asked me to write a document addressed to Avner and make clear some points. Gideon said it was very important. I was to state my opinion on the state of Israel and I was to state my feeling on how I felt about what Avner had done. He implied that he had no responsibility for what Avner might do. He wanted me to say how I felt about him and if I wanted to see him again. I began my letter saying that I loved Israel and that I was proud to be a Jew. I then said I thought Avner was super cool and was a hero, and that I wanted to see him again. I also made a comment saying I realized that he had done some bad things. I then said that I hoped one day Cindy would convert and maybe we would move to Israel. I told him Cindy did not know of my involvement in the murder. She did not know about the art dealer dying in Germany or the other Mossad agent who was set up by the Dutch prostitute, or Big Daddy the PLO drug dealer. You know we lived on less than five hundred U.S. a month. You know we were so young. Most of our time was consumed with buying groceries and cooking and taking our son to and from school. Gideon said he did not need her to sign the letter.

There were almost twenty agents in Woodstock that day. Gideon told me that some did not like Avner leaving the Mossad and were mad at him. Some supported him. It was like that. Everybody in Woodstock by now had heard about my exploits in Paris, and that bothered me. After all, I had a private life and it was supposed to be secret.

Woodstock was losing its appeal to me. Cindy wanted to stay. She loved her job. She worked in a clothing store called The Palace Museum. I wanted us to move to New York City. We fought about it. As a means of self-preservation I blocked these top secret espionage adventures out of my mind. As a means of self-preservation I refused to realize these things were happening.

Chapter Five

I did not want the Mossad to know where I was. I did not tell or want to talk about what happened in Paris. I found an apartment in Greenwich Village and I continued to do my art. I started a series of old Synagogues in Manhattan. Most of them were on streets in the Lower East Side, where there were heroin supermarkets. Right out on the street. There were guys grilling on fifty-gallon drums, music, prostitutes, lots of activity. I decided to do this series of old synagogues as a way to preserve Jewish culture and maybe to make some money. There were over a hundred synagogues in the Lower East Side that had at one time flourished and now were closed. Some were abandoned, some were sold to churches, and some were just left standing there. There was this artist who did sculpture that bought one of these old synagogues and made it into his studio and home.

I got a commission from one of the synagogues. I was asked, as part of a fund raising project to create a painting of Torah Scribes (a group of mostly men who resided in lower Manhattan and who created Torahs by hand) from this painting, I produced prints for their fundraiser. Their scrolls, which were made by hand, were on parchment from Israel. The pens were authentic, as was the ink. They were from a Hasidic sect, the Jews with the beards and long side burns. I met them and photographed them. Different synagogues would order Torahs from them. It was the Five Books of Moses in different scrolls. It took them over a year to do three of the five books. Synagogues spent over one hundred thousand for a set. I did paintings of them and then made a print of it. The

Memoirs of an Artist

synagogue commissioned me. These scribes were modern day Essenes.

Cindy got a job selling lingerie in the village. I tried to meet gallery owners and produce new work. Joshua went to school in the Little Red School house. That was a well known school that was in Greenwich village.

Robert Sheckley lived in the apartment above us. We became friends. He was a famous science fiction writer.

Cindy told me in the summer she wanted a trial separation when Joshua finished school. Joshua was going to stay with Bunny, Cindy's mother, during the summer. Cindy was to stay with a girlfriend and work in New York. In the fall, she said she did not want to get back together. She was moving to her mother's and commuting to Manhattan.

SELF PORTRAIT

Cindy and I worked hard to have a friendship

after we split up. Several years later she remarried and started a new family and lives near the Jersey shore. I stayed in the village. The Mossad was not after me at that moment but it was a dark period. I did beautiful renderings of crack houses.

By this time, I had changed my appearance. I did not look like a Biblical Prophet anymore. What women would want to kiss a guy whose beard smelled like fermented cheese? My taste was changing too. I did not want women who looked like they went to Grateful Dead concerts and did not shave their armpits and had hairy legs and dirty hair and dreadlocks. I found Republican women with big hair to be more attractive.

I was not aware of being followed or watched during that period. When I moved from Woodstock to Manhattan somebody told me Manhattan was the easiest and least expensive place to watch someone.

MY APARTMENT IN THE VILLAGE

I stayed in the village for another year. I always had a habit of making friends with Israelis. I bumped into an Israeli artist who I knew from the Ecole des Beaux art in Paris. His name was Aran. Was it a coincidence? We hung out. It seemed like every Israeli I met in Paris was Mossad. I guess he was too. A low level agent, army pay part time, very part time, almost like doing your country a favor. The Munich retaliation was still a high priority state secret. Not too many people outside of the group knew. I was still a top priority and they were afraid I would sell my story and embarrass them.

With all the experience I had with espionage in Europe I decided to put it to good use. I would go, for example, to Second Avenue Deli, order and eat. I would go into the restroom, change my hat and shirt, put on a fake moustache and leave the establishment.

I saved a bundle in those years getting over one hundred free meals. I learned how to eat in restaurants for free and duck out without paying.

After Cindy left me I found a new place to live. I knew a guy in Woodstock who had a gallery on Thompson Street. It had a nice apartment in the back. He decided to sublet it to me. I moved in my art and in a matter of days had opened a gallery. It was on Thompson between Houston and Bleeker.

My moods still fluctuated with the price of oil and Middle Eastern terrorist incidents. I was a man about town again. I knew people in all the neighborhoods.

I kept my mouth shut about Paris; I never wanted to write about my life in Paris with the rogue Mossad hit team. I continued to visit writers and got them to do stories on me in different publications about my art. I had an obsession about it. I never wanted to talk about Israel's state secrets. I did it to be a successful artist. I did get a certain amount of protection from the Mossad. I was so used to them pushing me around and my civil rights being violated. I was also selling my paintings, not a lot, but some. As far as women were concerned, I guess that was my form of self medication. I never drank and basically just smoked weed and hash. I met women all over town. For the most part, the only ones who would date me were from the slums or were art groupies. I remained friends with most. I was always honest, I just did not tell them that I did political assassinations on the side. I did keep doing paintings of Rubenesque nudes and indulge in sexual liaisons.

Chapter Six

My parents bought a farm in Newtown, Pa. Newtown was famous because George Washington slept there. It was settled before the revolutionary war. It was also home to Edward Hicks. He was a Quaker preacher and a famous artist. He was most well known for a series of paintings called the Peaceable Kingdom.

Twelve miles from Newtown was New Hope. New Hope is an art colony. It is on the
Delaware River. It is in Bucks County, Pennsylvania. Presently, it has a population of eight hundred people. Because of its abundance of water-power, the Indians considered it a sacred place. George Washington slept in New Hope also. Local legend has it that he had a mistress in town.

MY PAINTING OF
THE DELAWARE CANAL

At the turn of the century artists started to move there. It was inexpensive and naturally beautiful because of the river and many springs. Many of the artists had jobs teaching at the Pennsylvania Academy of Fine Arts in Philadelphia. It was commuting distance to New Hope.

There were mills located along these streams, and many of the artists were made famous by painting the mills and the Delaware River. In the 1930's, Harpo Marx, George Kaufmann and Moss Hart opened the Bucks County Playhouse which was on a mill along a stream that emptied into the Delaware River right in the center of the hamlet New Hope. It was also a center for handmade furniture, frame making, and arts and crafts.

There was a bridge in New Hope over the Delaware River which led to Lambertville which also had galleries and was not far from Trenton where I grew up. I knew people there, and a friend who had a gallery in Lambertville gave me a show. It was a way to escape the temptress Sophia, my current French girlfriend we had been living together in New York City

My parents let me stay on their farm in the caretaker cottage and work off the rent. That led to a contentious relationship with my father. He was never satisfied with my work. My mother was nice and we had a closer relationship. My relationship with my sister was pleasant but distant.

It was then that I began to teach. I had a lot of students and ran a small school offering art classes. The other single men in the area hated me because I had a lot of women friends. New Hope was in the country and in the country, because of farms, there are more Rubenesque women than you would find in a sophisticated place like Manhattan, where it was in vogue to be tall and thin.

I started doing Bucks County landscapes and garden scenes. They sold and I was able to save more money. This environment was healthy. I was not eating out of the garbage and I was producing a lot of new work.

I received a long distant call from Yael. She asked how I was and then told me she had to pay a private investigator one thousand dollars to find me. She wanted to know how I was coping. I said fine. Then she says don't you remember what we did. I said, with nonchalant, you mean when we went around and brought people from the French underground back to my apartment. She says yes. She was having a hard time coping from that and other things that happened. I did not know what she did after we lost touch in Paris. She did not know what I did when I hung with Gideon. It was a dirty war and she had post- traumatic stress and she said I should be having it too. I said I have moved on and did not think about it. She said I was insensitive and had no heart. She said that I did not recognize the magnitude of what we did. I said I wanted to move on and I was not affected. I just wanted to do my art and find a nice girl and settle down. She said I would never find someone. I was too damaged by what happened in Paris. She said she was too damaged as well. She said our partners could never understand what we did and how it affected us. Everyone who was associated with Operation Wrath of God was damaged. She then says she had a plan how we could make some money. She said she wanted to organize a tour where we would go to synagogues and speak. I could bring my art and dress up like a Mossad agent and do some role playing. I said I was not interested. I wanted to keep my secrets in my box. I did not want to spend the rest of my life living off what happened at Munich. She said I was going to have a major epiphany in the future.

At night I would drive twelve miles to New Hope. I would go to this nightclub called Havana's where I would meet my female art students... all at the same time. Life was more financially stable.

I had this one student who had written a book. She was a certified witch. She even had a diploma on her wall saying she went to a witch school. She was a minister in a secret female church which would meet late at night according to lunar cycles.

Wicca is a modern Pagan religion. It was developed in England during the first half of the twentieth century and it was introduced to the public in 1952 by Gerald Gardner, a retired British civil servant. Wicca draws upon a diverse set of ancient pagan and twentieth century hermetic motifs. For its structure and practice Wicca is typically dualistic-worshipping a God and Goddess, a mother Goddess, and a horned male God. Wicca celebrations are seasonally based festivals known as Sabbaths. Wicca involves the ritual practice of magic. My student's name was Sabrina She had written a book that was published privately about her participation in CIA experiments on a phenomenon called remote viewing. Sabrina was blond and tall and big in the hips. She told me that the witch history in Bucks County was very old. There were circles of witches in the area whose lineage went way back. They were called Covens. They were a small secret group. It was in the history of Bucks County that it was handed down from mother to daughter. It went back before the Revolutionary War. A lot of the original settlers came to escape persecution and some had unorthodox beliefs. The old stone houses in Bucks County had many ghosts in them.

The ghost of George Washington was spotted

many times around New Hope. George Washington had slept here. It was on the ghost tour. One drunken guy that saw it claimed that George had his pants down at the old stone house in town. He was rumored to have a mistress in New Hope. Sabrina told me a meeting was coming up on the full moon. The witch's house belonged to a woman named Debbie. She had a boyfriend, an artist, who was a friend of mine. His name was Dmitri. Debbie's family had lived in that old stone house for generations.

The night of the meeting, under a tight veil of secrecy, we all arrived forty- five minutes before midnight. There were twelve people in attendance. Each person represented one month of the year - six men and six women. There was a fire going in the hearth. It was a large fireplace that was built out of stone and ran the length of the kitchen. The ceilings were low. Large wooden beams ran across the ceiling. The house was prerevolutionary war. We all exchanged greetings and warmed ourselves by the fire. It was the middle of the winter and there had been a blizzard the day before. No snow had melted. We all had chains and snow tires on our cars.

We began removing our clothing because the room was very hot. We began singing, but it was more like a sacred chanting as we began shedding more clothes. We were down to our underwear and the chanting continued.

We swayed, our shoulders touched warm skin to warm skin, as the singing took us to another place. We were all high from the rhythm of the singing. Touching gave way to hugging. There was an even match between men and women. Witches tend to be fat and have brooms. I was in heaven. Hugging gave way to light kissing and drinking sacred wine which had been poured and blessed.

When the singing stopped, we all went outside got naked and rolled around in the snow. After we rolled around in the snow, when everyone was getting dressed, all the women were making jokes about the six old fashioned brooms that were there. They said they were going to get home with their brooms by air rather than by car.

Before the ceremony had started, not long after we had arrived, a circle had been drawn around the room with white chalk. And so to end the ceremony, we stood within this circle, protected from the evil spirits, holding hands, and chanted one more time. This was the life style of that time. People were really into new age science. I was a follower of those trends and it influenced my art. Besides being fascinated with Wicca I also had a fascination with pyramids. They started to appear in my drawings and paintings.

FLOATING PYRAMIDS

I went to Egypt twice and painted the pyramids on these month long trips. (The Egyptian Pyramids are ancient pyramid structures.) There are 138 pyramids in Egypt. Most of them are tombs for the pharaohs and their consorts.

The estimate of the numbers of workers who built these structures ranges from a few thousand to over a hundred thousand. The most famous of these pyramids are at Giza, a suburb of Cairo. Several of the pyramids are counted among the largest structures ever built.

The pyramid Khufu at Giza is the largest. It is the only one built that was considered one of the Seven Wonders of the World.

The first trip my goal was to do paintings of the pyramids. I also went by horseback from the pyramids in Giza to Saqqarah which was a thirty- mile trip.

We passed by smaller lesser known pyramids which were my favorites. I like one called the "bent pyramid," and some of the smaller ones. The thing I liked about Egypt was that the men did not like skinny women. They were considered both poor and sickly. Overweight women were considered healthy and rich, getting enough to eat.

I stayed at a hotel by Khan Khalili. It was next to the slave market. The hash market was around the corner. Talk about alleyways and water pipes, I felt right at home. I would take a bus or cab to the pyramids every day and work, plein air. I had enough money to hire an assistant.

My favorite view of the pyramids was from the south. That required a horseback ride up dunes that were the size of ski slopes. Once at the viewing spot there would be a camel and Bedouin tent. Tea was ten in the morning and three in the afternoon.

My hotel at the old slave market had some Danish architects staying there. They were in Cairo renovating an old palace in the historic part of town. One of the architects was an attractive tall Danish redhead. We instantly connected. Her name was Inga. Inga had large bosoms and was wide at the hips and tall.

DRAWING OF THE PYRAMIDS

A love affair in a spy den like Cairo was a great aphrodisiac. We explored the places off the tourist map and planned a rendezvous, where she always talked about, in the south of Egypt.

Islamic fundamentalism was just beginning to blossom at that time. That was something I was really against. I liked it that Egyptian men liked big women. I did not tell anyone that I was Jewish. People in Egypt did not like Israelis or Jewish people in particular.

On one more of these trips to Egypt, I took my son out of school and he came with me. That's when I first went south. We took the train to Aswan. There are more varieties of bird and fish there than anywhere in the world.

We saw Elephantine Island where there were ancient settlements of Jews.

Our plan was to rent a small fishing boat and sail north to Luxor. The trip was illegal now because some tourists had disappeared some months earlier. It was rumored they were eaten by some hungry Egyptians from some poor villages.

We made our deal in Aswan. We were going to be smuggled a few miles north to meet our boat and crew. We left at sunset, hiding under some blankets. At ten at night, by candlelight, we were transferred to our boat and met our crew. One was a cook and one was the captain. We sailed north reaching the ruins of Komombo the next afternoon.

Seeing this ancient temple from the period of the Pharaohs' in late afternoon light, on a boat on the Nile is a sight to behold. It was then that I lit up my hash pipe and smiles erupted from the crew. They did not speak English. They just said "Hubbely Bubblely." Two more days and nights on the boat and it seemed like my son and I were speaking fluent Nubian. We stopped at a mud village to buy meat off a half a cow hanging on a hook. There were millions of flies all around. I also bought some more hash.

We had a big communal meal out of a large dish that everybody ate with their fingers. The women were all covered. It was hot enough we were wearing shorts and tee shirts. One woman who was caught looking at us was severely whipped by her older brother. That happened right in front of my son and me. It was then that I had a premonition of 9/11. It was a relief when we reached Luxor. There was even more drama there. We made friends with an Egyptian tour guide who would not let us talk to other Egyptians and kept us prisoners.

He also took us to this hotel on the other side of the Nile that was in an old farmhouse. We were made to feel like prisoners. Our tour guide's name was none other than Mohammed. He took us to these secret caves by Valley of the Kings. We were allowed to help ourselves to old mummies that were in there. I brought a few heads home.

When that trip ended we went back to my parents' farm. Shortly afterwards, my son Joshua moved into the farm with me. Cindy's mother was selling her house. Cindy was moving into her new boyfriend's house.

I would always get these phone calls that I did not understand and I could not process. They involved Paris. The American Mercenary still called. I got a call from him and his wife. I think it was the last time he called before he and his wife died. I did mention earlier in this story that one of the Israeli hit squad was an American. He was a Vietnam vet; he was not Jewish. They were in Hollywood at the home of a famous actress known for her sympathy for protests and left wing causes. They said they were working on a screen play about the Munich aftermath, would I help. I froze as I always did, in disbelief and confusion. I could not connect with them about that. There were too many things I did not understand and I wanted to keep all things about Paris in my secret box. and they seemed irritated. They commented on how my trauma in Paris had caused amnesia and that it was too bad. This Hollywood actress, that was on the phone, said the story about my amnesia was more interesting than the Munich story. She said that if it was true, I had a great story. The famous Hollywood actress then said she heard that I was a really cool artist and it was too bad I could not help. She then called me an asshole and hung up.

I was still being watched by the Mossad. They did not want the story of their operation being revealed by anyone, especially me.

I had a gallery on Ney Alley in a tree house built by famed woodworker Jeffry Green. Ney alley was named after Bill Ney, a famous artist, who studied in Paris and later made New Hope his home in 1927. At the end of the Ney Alley was Mechanic Street. On Mechanic stood the Arts Works, a building that was just for galleries. Every other building on that street was a gallery of some sort. The other buildings were restaurants. Mechanic Street had a lot of history. There was a ghost tour that took place in New Hope and most of the tour was on Mechanic Street. The earliest building on the corner was built in 1690 and it had a ghost seen by its present occupants. The ghost had clothing on from that period.

The Art Works building had two apartments on the top floor. A writer had moved in there. He was an Israeli who drove around the country doing stories on Americans.

He showed up in town in an old broken down car that barely ran. He wore a worn tweed jacket with patches on its sleeves. His pants were tattered but they were neatly pressed. He was short, slightly overweight, gentle-looking, but slightly odd. I would call him a nebbish. He was well kept, in a poor sort of way. He needed a lot of dental work, (which to me, was a giveaway about being a bum.)

He wanted to see my gallery because he was doing stories on artists.

I told him I had many Israeli friends and had emotional ties to Israel. I said I supported Labour and not Likud. He was a Likudnik, and we would have conversations about politics in Israel. Sometimes one of us would get a little excited. One day we were discussing the case of Mordechai Vanunu, the Israeli who was caught selling secrets of Israel's secret atomic bomb plant in Dimona, Israel. The Israelis caught him in a yacht off the coast of Australia. He was lured in and captured by a beautiful Mossad agent who went to his yacht to smoke hash.

Vanunu worked in a plant in Dimona, Israel. He

then sold the secrets to a British tabloid about Israel having the bomb, and high tailed it to Australia on a yacht. My argument was from the liberal side, and this writer whose name was David, took a more conservative stance. My point of view was that you could still be a loyal Israeli and support Mordecai Vanunu. His decision to rat out a secret illegal project, basically made him a whistle blower. The plutonian was secretly smuggled out of a private plant in America and sold illegally to Israel for their secret bomb factory.

Some supported this; some did not. So, anyway, David the nebbish and I had a big argument about it, and I accused him of being a Mossad agent. The next day he left town without saying goodbye to anyone. He was a Mossad agent and he probably worked for a couple of hundred a month. He was hired by my friend Gideon to find out what I was doing. Apparently he had some kind of crisis after our argument about Dimona.

I went to my gallery one day and there was a small note on my door. The message said that he was a friend of Gideon and he was coming to see me. It was very important that I be there at one o'clock. At one I arrived, he was with his charming and attractive wife. He was a middle aged, very buff, high-level agent. He was with the Israeli consulate in Manhattan.

He said he was checking me out because David quit his job; he told the Mossad he left to go back to Israel because of emotional reasons. He asked me how I knew he was an agent. I told him I have met so many I can spot them in a second. I told him he took notes with the same pad and pencil that Gideon used. Also, the arm patches on his sport coat were a dead giveaway Mossad uniform. Moreover, he had the same golf hat as Gideon.

He tells me I am being watched; the Operation

Wrath of God is still state secret. It will go public in a year and a half. I have to be careful never to talk about it because it could affect the security for the state of Israel. I show them my art. It was like a dream. If the Mossad would have stopped reminding me, I would have forgotten about it. He went on to tell me something.... another thing that went into my box of secrets. The Mossad spent more money following me than they did in its entire history of following people. I guess I should be grateful they didn't just kill me. That they value human life enough to spend all that money following a left wing Jewish artist who was a pot head and liked Rubenesque women. That's why the Israeli government trades thousands of Palestinian prisoners for one soldier. That's why America supports Israel because our values are the same.

    I got this really weird phone call. The man introduced himself as an official from the Israeli government. He asked if I knew a General Zvi Samir from Paris. I said yes. He said that there was a lady there who wanted to talk to me. It was Golda Meir, the Prime Minister of Israel. It was the day of a ceremony that marked the end of her project operation Wrath of God (the revenge for the murdered Israelis at Munich), being a state secret. Before she got on the phone, this official said he was going to hand the phone over to her. Something snapped in me. I was so traumatized, brow beaten, threatened, followed, had my civil rights violated, that I had had enough! When this official told me that Golda was getting on the phone, I told the guy that I did not believe him. Why was he playing this joke on me after everything that happened? He said well what did the Mossad do to you, I said they were always moving my art around and hiding it. They would put rotten grapes on my chair and I would sit on them... things like that. Well when

Golda got on the phone, I was so sure this was all a practical joke that I hung up. The official called back and thought that the line went dead due to technical problems. He told me that I just hung up on Golda Meir. I still did not believe him. A short time later I got a call from Yael. She said she was at the ceremony. It was a grey day. The leader Avner refused to attend. He was living in the states. It was not a happy time many people had died. Some soldiers laughed when I hung up on the Prime Minister; they were reprimanded. I found out later that Gideon and the other generals laughed at the officers' club afterwards, while having drinks ...for two years about my antics. And that I was famous in Israel with a lot of the top generals and spies from that era.

When my son was thirteen my parents planned to take us to Israel for his Bar Mitzvah. We had it on Masada. We went with a group from our synagogue from Trenton, New Jersey. Our Rabbi came with us as well as his married girlfriend. He was married too. A Bar Mitzvah is a service where a young man at the age of thirteen becomes a man. He reads from the Torah, Jewish Holy books, leads a service, and is officially in full standing as a Jew. It was a very emotional service and tears were shed. Joshua's had to memorize along Torah portion. He performed it well. He also learned Hebrew, and did a good job reading some prayers before and after his Torah portion.

Joshua's mother was a gentile, so a year before going on the trip we had a ceremony where Joshua was dunked into the Delaware River. This was a Jewish kind of Baptism. Before that he had his penis pricked by a Moil. A moil is a man that performs a circumcision. Joshua was circumcised at the time of his birth, so what he had done was just ceremonial. The other people in the group were a few elderly widows from my temple, my parents and my son.

We toured the country in a rented tour bus along with a driver and a tour guide. We saw the whole country. We did parts of Sinai, we went to Elot in the south, next to Aquaba in Jordan. We travelled to Haifa and the Golan Heights. Over the course of a few weeks we saw the whole country.

Masada is an ancient formation in the southern desert on top of an isolated rock plateau upon the eastern edge of the Judean Desert. Herod the Great built it in thirty-seven to thirty-one B.C. Several years later, during a war with the Romans, nine hundred and sixty Jewish rebels committed suicide rather than surrender to the Roman army. When a young man or woman enters the army it is a tradition that he or she climb it with their full army gear.

The day of my sons Bar Mitzvah we all climbed to the top of this plateau at Masada. The older people that were with us took a tram to the top. I thought the climb up was easy. There was a young Israeli soldier doing the climb with a backpack.

While our service was going on, a rare thing happened. We heard thunder. In Biblical days, thunder was the sound of the Lord. It rarely rained there, and after the thunder we got some sprinkles.

Our visit to Jerusalem was the most moving and emotional part of our journey. The story of Jerusalem tells a lot of the story of the Israeli Palestinian conflict. I did several paintings of Jerusalem on that trip and sold them on the spot. During its long history Jerusalem has been destroyed twice, besieged twenty- three times, and attacked fifty-two times. It was captured and recaptured forty- four times.

**MY PAINTING OF
THE WAILING WALL**

The oldest part of the city was settled in the fourth millennium making Jerusalem the oldest city in the world. According to the Bible, the Israelites history in the city began in one thousand BC with King David's sacking of the city. Following this, Jerusalem became the city of David and capital of the United Kingdom of Israel.

Later, according to Biblical narratives, King Solomon built a more substantial temple.

I spent days wandering the alleys and labyrinths of the old city. I split off from the tour group and was on my own. I took in all the smells in the markets, of the spices, and the blood of freshly slaughtered animals. Some alleys had the scent of danger; others bustled with the noise of commerce.

Billy Selesnick

**SELF PORTRAIT
IN THE OLD CITY**

Whispering was common with the Arab merchants. The streets echoed with the sound of Israeli army units on foot patrol.

There were two highlights of this trip. One was Masada for Joshua's Bar Mitzvah and the other was my trip to the Wailing or Western Wall. The Western Wall or Wailing Wall is located in the Old City of Jerusalem, at the foot of the Western side of the Temple Mount. It's remnant of the ancient wall that surrounds the large Jewish courtyard, and it's arguably, the most sacred site of Jewish people.

When visiting the wall for my first time, I prayed there. It's a custom to write down a prayer on a small piece of paper, roll it up, and then put it in between the cracks of the stones. The bottom stones are very large and people always wondered how they moved these giant stones into place and piled them one on top of another.

When there, I took some photographs of people praying at the wall. I immediately started painting from them upon arriving home. I painted dozens of scenes of people at the wall. I painted them in umber to capture the light. The light in Jerusalem is unlike any light I have seen in the world. It has been a site of Jewish prayer and pilgrimage for centuries. Outbreaks of violence have been common with the rise of Zionism.

I painted plein air on top of Mount of Olives. I did a very detailed pencil drawing of the Old City with the Dome of the Rock that was in the center.

The Dome of the Rock is a shrine located at the Temple Mount in the Old City Of Jerusalem. The structure has been refurbished many times since its completion in the year 691 BC, at the order of Umayyad Caliph Block-Malik.

The sign fence of this site stems from a religious tradition regarding the rock known as The Fountain Stone. It is at its heart. Legend has it that this site was also where Mohammed went up to heaven. It was also the site where Abraham on the order of God was told to sacrifice his first born Isaac.

The location was established as the site of Islam and the miracle of Isra and Neray by Caliph Omarbin al Khatab, who was advised by his associate, a former Jewish rabbi that converted to Islam, that this stone was part of a tradition of a Night Journey which took place at this site.

Halfway through the trip, at a restaurant in Jerusalem, a man approached me and said "remember me?" It was Steve. He said the old man wanted to see what I was doing there (meaning Gideon wanted to know why I was in Israel). He was pissed off and wanted to know what I was doing in Egypt on these long trips. Certain segments in Israel feel it's disloyal for a Jew to visit an Arab country before Israel. They were wondering if I was nefarious. They thought maybe I was up to no good, like political stuff.

Actually, I was ashamed for not visiting Israel first. At the same time, I was defiant. I broke no laws by doing that. As a matter of fact, I saw the ugliness first hand of Islamic fundamentalism, when that girl got whipped for looking at us. Steve said when he was driving to the restaurant, he was wondering if he was going to have to arrest me. I said for what? I said I was in Egypt doing paintings of the pyramids. Maybe it was disloyal to spend so much time in Egypt, a former enemy of Israel. I was still a naive artist, and did not think it was disloyal to go to Egypt first. Finally, he accepted my explanation of why I was in Egypt then he asked me to buy him a beer. I did, and he wanted to know what I had been doing. Then he said what happened in Paris was now public knowledge. He now had a very important job that had something to do with the security of the state of Israel. His reward for a job well done.

The old man was still concerned about what happened to me in Paris. He was worried that I never got therapy after what happened. The people that don't get therapy usually end up being considered unstable and a walking time bomb.

I still wanted to keep those memories in that box. He asked me if I read the Jonas book. I had not at that time. I still did not know the full extent to which I was involved. I did not want to know. I did not want to watch out for Palestinians my whole life.

Then he asked me if I had sex with any women when I was in Israel. He said it would not be a crime if I had. I knew better than trying to lie. I told him I had a fling with a bartender at a kibbutz where we had stayed. He asked me if I had any diseases. I said I hope not. I didn't, thank God. He asked me if I wanted her to visit in the states, and I said yes. We shook hands when he left. Steve, the Mossad agent who I hung out with in Paris, Steve, who I was with when we were shot at. Steve, the guy I searched for information for at Montmartre. Steve, the guy who I was with when we both posed as rock stars, in search of PLO sympathizers. Steve, the guy with the gun in his belt outside Montmartre. He then said that I could visit Gideon, if I wanted to. He said his ex-girlfriend, Yael, would like to hear from me. Then we shook hands. His hands had an eerie feeling; they were frigid.

    My time in Israel was an emotional experience. We visited Yad Voshem, the holocaust museum, and it was a moving experience. Several distant relatives had perished in the Nazi holocaust. I was trying to move on from my experiences with the Mossad in Paris and its aftermath. I never visited Gideon. I was in a state of shock. Steve said Gideon would have come to meet our tour group but he was not feeling well. I did not visit Yael and she was very pissed off about it. She told me in a phone call a year later. This trip to Israel did little to shake the sense of denial and amnesia about what happened to me in Paris. Looking back I realize I was in far deeper then I remember.

    Shortly afterwards, we returned to the states. A month later the Israeli girl, the bartender from the Kibbutz, came to visit. After we made love, she told me that the Mossad agent came to visit her and they wanted information about me. They told her they thought I was a big drug dealer. They didn't tell her too much, but what they did say was to watch out for anything she thought was weird. She told me she reacted negatively to what they said, out of loyalty to me. She stayed a week or two then she moved on to visit another friend. She then overstayed her visit and got in hot water because of it. Apparently, Golda Meir had approved her coming over and her visa application was rushed through.

I got this strange threatening phone call from a woman with an Israeli accent. She wanted to know why I was not marrying the girl who had been staying with me. The girl's name was Miriam. I said we were just friends, and the lady got mad at me and said she was going to come over and teach me a lesson. She said she was living in New York. I said, look I am just an artist. She said I had something to do with Munich, but she did not know what.

Then she mentioned the Prime Minister's name and I was dumbstruck.

I was approached by a person who wanted to know my views on the Middle East. He told me he was writing a book and he was an historian. He was a well-dressed gentleman. He had dark skin. I felt he was P.L.O. He looked very smart and effete.

I saw the movie Munich on TV. I had chills when I saw it, and had flashbacks. I put them in that box. The same thing happened when I saw the TV documentary Sword of Gideon.

In 1982, Israel invaded Lebanon to crush out terrorism inflicted on Israel and Jews around the world. As usual, the whole world was against Israel. This was due to the fact that Israel was overly aggressive in their retaliation against terrorism, because innocent civilians got caught in the crossfire. I watched the news nonstop, even when there were no wars. So this had my attention. Studying Israel and the Jews was a lifelong obsession. I am a leftist, but

Israel was an exception. All my leftist friends were against Israel. I was for Israel.

Once I got a call from a woman who wanted me to comment on a movie that was made. I pretended to not understand what she was talking about. She said my character was in it. When I said that I did not know what she was talking about she said hold on. Another person came to the phone. This was a male voice and he said he knew me from Paris back in the day. I came out of my amnesia-like state. He said what drugs are you on. I said I just smoke pot and he said I was acting like I was on something much stronger. He said that because I was acting so unaware about what happened in Paris. Then another guy got on the phone who said he knew me from Paris too, back in 1976, and he wanted to know what was going on in my life. Then I was told that Yael had told her story. She felt that she had been ignored. Not included in the Munich movie, she never made any money but everyone else had. Now it was her turn. This new movie that was opening in New York, was made in Hebrew and had English subtitles.

Around this time, Avner's mother came to visit me in my gallery. She was opening a gift shop and wanted to see my paintings. Then I talked to Avner on the phone. I was considered his responsibility because he had brought me in. He said that I should get therapy. I said that no shrink would believe me about working with the Mossad. Then I told him, I did not know who I was because I was so confused about why so many people were always following me. I told him I did not know who I was because I did not remember what I did. At this point I was yelling and crying at the famous Avner. I was flipping out on him. He tried to be nice and said that I was not the only person who got hurt from that era. I said I had no training for what happened to me. I said I had already had a screw loose before I went to Paris.

Avner said he hoped our families could be friends. I had blown it when his mother visited me in my gallery. I was not as composed as Avner, and I felt I was not as sophisticated as him. Anyway, our conversation ended with his advice, to read and study about that era and maybe one day we could talk in the future.

I was living then in New Hope where I had a gallery and was making money. At least enough money to maintain the gallery and take long exotic vacations. I never saved anything.

I was good at getting write-ups. I was a publicity addict. I had never even thought about Munich nor the boys. I got well known without them. I would get these other calls from people who said they were screenwriters and I always pretended I did not know what they were talking about.

One day this very attractive women came into my gallery. Her name was Nina. She was Israeli. She tells me she's an artist who went to art school in Israel and that she also was in the Mossad for a few years. She was looking for a job in the states in the security business. Avner, when he moved to the states, was also in the security business and she had applied for a job there. At least that was the impression I got. She was checking my art out. I was checking her out. She tells me her specialty in the Mossad was martial arts. She was drop dead beautiful and looked really smart. I immediately thought that Avner sent her to use her to get information about me. Was I talking to writers?

BILLY WORKING ON A MURAL

Was I talking to famous movie stars who heard about my exploits? She then wanted to know how I knew Avner. She asked me if I knew he was a major superhero and legend. I said I knew. The only thing I told her that afternoon was that over ten people had threatened to kill me. She said it must be hard living with what happened to you. This woman had the potential to be a real Femme Fatal. Maybe even a Mata Hari.

The real Mata Hari was born Margreet MacLeod in Holland in 1876. She was a Dutch Frisian exotic dancer and courtesan, who was convicted of being a spy and executed by firing squad in France under charges of espionage for Germany in World War One. In 1903 she moved to Paris where she was a circus horse rider. She also modeled for artists. In 1905 she won fame as an exotic dancer. Promiscuous, flirtatious and openly flaunting her body, Mata Hari became an overnight success.

BILLY'S NEW WIFE

The idea of an exotic dancer working as a lethal double agent, using her power of seduction to extract military secrets from her many lovers made Mata Hari the enduring arch type of the femme fatal. Nina was a real Mata Hari.

Shortly afterwards, I met a woman who was born in Florence, Italy. Her mother was a countess related to the Borgheses. Her father was half British/half American, and he met my future wife's mother when he was stationed in Florence during World War II. He was an ambulance driver during the war. They returned to the states and moved to New Hope when she was five years old. Her name was Artemisia and

English was her second language.

Her father was an artist, an oil painter. He loved these painters who lived around Florence and who painted in a style similar to the Impressionists. He also had a great love for opera and later became a well known opera impresario. He bought a lot of my paintings and was a great friend.

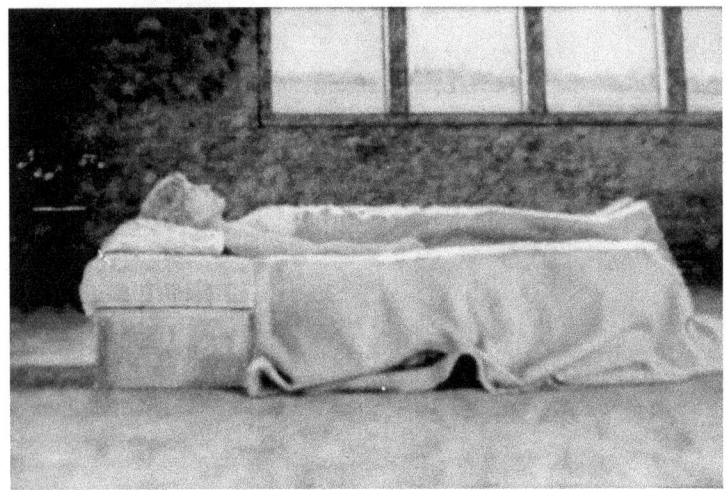

ARTEMISIA DAY DREAMING

He named his daughter Artemisia after a woman artist who was a contemporary of Caravavaggio. Artemisia was considered one of the finest women artists from that time. She lived from 1593 to 1656. In those days women stayed home and had kids. She was a rarity. She was the first woman who was accepted into the painting academy in Florence. There was an incident where she was raped by some male students and she testified against them in court. Today she is considered a source of inspiration in the Women's movement in Italy.

Artemisia returned to Florence when she finished high school. She went to study art restoration at the same academy that the original Artemisia studied. When finished she came back to New Hope and opened a jewelry shop called Room at the Top.

I met her when she came into Karla's restaurant. I was renovating a room there, painting faux marble walls and a sky ceiling. A mutual friend brought her in to see it. Artemisia loved art.

She was a natural beauty. Men would come on to her all the time. She was partners in her store with her ex boyfriend named Chuck. He was an ex football player and very protective of her. That made it difficult for suitors to come around. He was away on vacation when we met. We had a whirlwind romance and were an item by the time he returned. We were probably exact opposites. She dressed meticulously. I dressed like a homeless bum. I was always covered in paint. She thought about things before doing them. I was totally impulsive. She cooked and ate slow, I cooked and ate fast. She wanted to make love slowly and I was like a jackrabbit.

From the start we would fight about Chuck. I was jealous and insecure. I felt that she spent more time with him than me. I did not like going into her store. We did however have important things in common. We shared many mutual interests. We both loved classical music. We loved art and art history, books, walking the beach or by the Delaware River. I enjoyed painting her. We got married and went to Israel for our honeymoon and had a son right away. I never told her about what happened to me in Paris. That is how deep it was in my box.

In Jerusalem during our honey moon I was approached by a man who said he worked for security. I asked Shin Bet? He said he wanted to know what we were doing because of the stamps in my passport. My wife, a countess from Florence, did not know my past.

Memoirs of an Artist

We took the bus from Jerusalem to Cairo. We drove by the Gaza strip and saw the most crowed place in the world, Gaza City.

We passed over to the Egyptian side and got on a different bus. We ended up having a night or two at the Mena House by the pyramids. It's an old palace that was converted into a hotel. Churchill, Truman and Stalin had a meeting there during World War II.

Before we flew home we traveled back to Israel the same way. This time at the border crossing, on the Israeli side, they found a gun in the suitcase of one of the locals. I told Artemisia about my thing for big women. She reacted the same way my first wife did, with amusement. However, an affair with a skinny woman would be met with instantaneous divorce, as I was soon to find out.

When we returned to New Hope I became more well-known. I was making money through my art and going on these wild trips for a year to different places. I moved my beautiful wife and family to Negril, Jamaica where I painted for a year on the beach.

Chapter Seven

Jamaica is an island country situated in the Caribbean Sea. It is the third largest island of the greater Antilles. The island is 4,240 square miles and lies ninety miles south of Cuba. The indigenous people, the Taino, called it Xaymaca in Arawakan, meaning the "Land of Wood and Water" or "Land of Springs." Jamaica was once a Spanish possession known as Santiago. In 1655 it became a possession of England and was called Jamaica. It achieved full independence from England in 1962. With two million five hundred thousand people, it is the third most populist Anglophone country in the Americas. Kingston is its capital and largest city. Jamaica has a large diaspora around the world. Today Jamaica is mostly known for its reggae music. It is also a haven for those whose passions lie with the smoking of cannabis.

Actually the reason we picked Jamaica to move to started with my oldest son Joshua. He was a big fan of reggae and had dreadlocks. (That's when your hair gets long and becomes matted together.) He turned me onto reggae and I soon became a fan as well.

Joshua was a good student in public school and had entered the honors program for gifted students. My father, after seeing Joshua's entry into the honor program, decided in ninth grade to put him into the George School, an expensive Quaker private prep school located in Newtown. The campus was like a college campus in the country. It had many old historic buildings and many of the students were children of wealthy people and celebrities.

Joshua was an honor roll student and star player on the football team. The summer of ninth grade he got

Memoirs of an Artist

overly involved with a girl from the area. He also started smoking a lot of weed. He kind of started spiraling down that summer. When he began tenth grade, he did not want to play football anymore and was into the Rastafarian philosophy. His grades also spiraled down that year. He became suicidal. I promised him, if he finished school that year we would move to Jamaica for a long trip. I told him he could be home schooled there. Anyway, on the second to last day of school that year he was caught smoking pot and thrown out. I mean school was all ready over. It just meant he could not go back the next year. We were going to be in Jamaica anyway.

The Rastafarians intrigued me. The Rastafarian movement is a spiritual movement that arose in 1930 in Jamaica. Its' adherent worship, Haille Selassis, of Ethiopia lived from 1930 to 1974. Some of the Rastafarians worship him as Jesus Incarnate, others as God, or the Father. The name Rastafaria is taken from "ras" and "tafari," the preregal name of the title, Haille Sellasie. Many elements of Rastafarianism reflect its origins in Jamaica, which is a country with ninety-eight percent black descendants of slaves.

The Movement of Rastafarianism encompasses things such as the spiritual use of cannabis and the rejection of western society referred to as Babylon. It proclaims Africa as the birthplace of man. A central theme in Rastafarianism is the return to Africa. Rastafarianism is not a highly organized religion. It is a movement, it is an ideology, and it is a way of life. They felt connected to Ethiopia and Haille Selassie. He was from the same bloodline as King David. In their art they had Jewish symbols and pictures of the lion of Judah. Many people think the Ark of the Covenant is in an old church in Ethiopia. Everybody knows about all the Ethiopian Jews that were air lifted to Israel.

Billy Selesnick

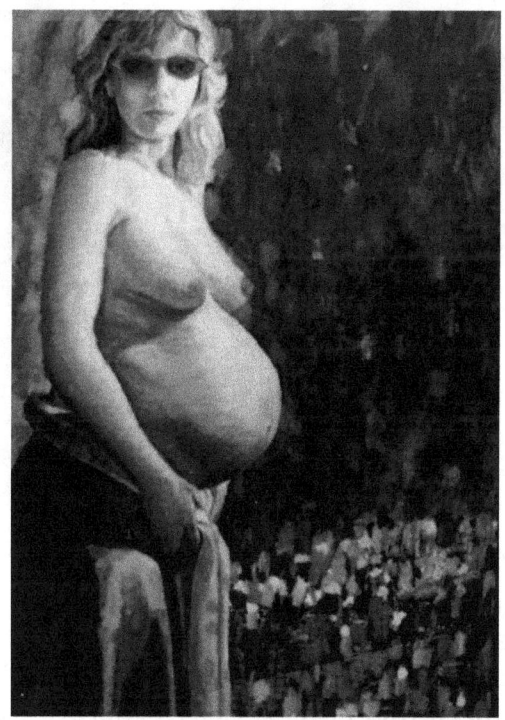

ARTEMISIA PREGNANT WITH REMBRANDT

Artemisia and Joshua never liked each other. Joshua was jealous of Artemisia and vice versa. Around this time Artemisia and I had a son. His name was Rembrandt. We named after an artist who was born in 1483 and lived to 1520. Rembrandt was an Italian painter and one of the leaders of the high Renaissance.

When Rembrandt was born we got an au pair from Florence, Italy, the place of my wife's birth.

When it was time to move to Jamaica, Artemisia, our son Jason, and the au pair went to Florence. Artemisia joined us in Jamaica a few months later.

We moved to Jamaica about two weeks after hurricane Gilbert. The island had been devastated.

SEVEN MILE BEACH

Joshua and I got an apartment in Negril where there is a seven-mile beach. Negril is a small country town that started as a poor fishing village. When we arrived, there was no electricity. There were also no tourists and no food. Even water was scarce. People were living from the coconuts. There was a hooker population in Negril and there were no johns. I found that out when I went to an almost deserted nightclub on our third night there. Over the course of a few months the island was rebuilt, and then the tourists started coming back to town.

Joshua's home schooling turned out to be a disaster. His French teacher turned out to be a French crackhead, and was taking my money and buying crack. She then tried to seduce my son. My son then fell in with a bunch of teenage ragamuffins. They convinced him to run away from me and move in with them.

By the time Artemisia arrived with our son Rembrandt, Joshua had disappeared and we rarely saw him. If we ever did, it was when he needed money.

I painted a lot there, and when the tourists came back I was able to make a good living from selling my work. I did sunset paintings, boat paintings, and the beach night scenes. I also did a lot of portraits.

**JAMAICAN SUNSET
OIL ON BOARD**

When Artemisia and Rembrandt arrived we moved to the Tree House Hotel which is on the beach. I became friendly with the owner, and for part of the time we rented a giant suite. We got a special price and I paid a monthly rate.

There were a lot of zaftig women there. There were a lot of Jamaican women who liked tourists. There was the wildest night life there that I have ever seen anywhere. Going out at night to these Reggae shows was really a trip. They started really late. Every night in Negril there would be a different hot spot, On Friday night all the action would be at the cliffs. That's where the water came up to the cliffs and there would be no beach. On Saturday night the action would be at De Bus, a club on the beach. On Sunday, the action could be at a disco in the center of town. That was called the Roundabout and so on and so on. Jamaicans would get really dressed up for these affairs. The tourists would come in different styles. Some would get dressed up and some would go ragamuffin style. A lot of people would be smoking weed and doing coke at these shows. There would be little six year- old boys selling peanuts. The thing about Jamaican people that amazed me was how they moved. They were some of the best dancers in the world.

Every Jamaican man's dream is to seduce a white woman, especially one with blond hair. Seduction became an art down there. White women would come from all over the world for what was known as "black bamboo." Rasta men were adept at having harems composed of white women. It was not unusual for a black Rasta guy to have different white women all over the island. White guys would come to Jamaica with their white girlfriends or wife, and the second the white guy would turn around, his wife or girlfriend would be seduced by a black Rasta guy. These reggae shows were the places where these liaisons would manifest. There were also many black prostitutes at these shows. They would solicit mostly white guys because they were the ones with the money. Jamaican women who were not prostitutes were usually conservative and family oriented. Before my wife Artemisia came down, I had some affairs with some tourists that I met through doing portraits. I also had some relationships with some buxom Jamaican women. I had never been with black women before this. At these reggae shows there could be a lot of fights. Usually they were over white women or drug deals.

Jamaica was very poor. The drug culture exasperated the situation. Farmers were growing cannabis, the cash crop, instead of food. That created food shortages and high prices. At the supermarket everything that was imported was expensive.

BOATS

Jamaica had the reputation of being dangerous and that there was a lot of crime. Most of the crime was drug related and there was a lot of robbery. In Jamaica, if you were white you got hassled a lot. That meant every time you were walking around, Jamaicans would follow you and try to sell you something. A lot of people, when they moved about, would need to have body guards. I got hassled a lot but was never robbed. I was always a target because I made money from selling my art, and all the Jamaicans knew it.

There was a lot of political violence between the different political parties. This violence would erupt around the time of Jamaican elections.

When we first arrived in Jamaica, I would go to this café on the beach called The Office. It was a few miles from where my son and I were renting an apartment. I used to like to go there at night. This café had a group of hustlers that used to hang out there and play cards and gamble. Some pimps and prostitutes hung out there as well. One night, when it was time for me to walk home, this prostitute named Peaches followed me. On the way home, on the beach, which was very dark, she was begging me for action. I did not know it, but several pimps were following us and their plan was, when she seduced me and my pants were down, they were going to jump out from the bushes and rob me.

There was a lot of reverse racism. A lot of black Jamaicans did not like whites. The island was probably ninety percent black. The other ten percent were mixed-Whites with some black blood, Indians and Asians. The lighter your skin usually meant you had more money.

The Asians and Indians usually were from the merchant class and owned a lot of the motels and hotels. White tourists who fell in love with the island and wanted to stay, had a hard time making money. I became a target because I was one of the white guys who could make money. I was also a target with the hookers, because they knew I had money.

Jamaica was the drug capital of the world. Big grass and coke dealers were all over the island. I sold paintings to a lot of them. I was taken to big marijuana plantations all over the island. I even did and sold paintings of cannabis. Most of these cannabis farms were in the country, not near the beach. They were in the hills where the Rastas kept their white women. I did not sell weed or drugs when I was in Jamaica. I did not have to. I made enough from my art.

I ended up living in Jamaica for two years. It was a very exotic and beautiful place. When we left Jamaica, we lived in Key West for a while. I had a premonition about a future in Key West, and ten years later moved back there for seven years.

Chapter Eight

My wife still had a store in New Hope. Her partner ran it while she had been in Jamaica. It was 1990. So we eventually went back to town and I opened another gallery. I loved my wife, but I was insecure and had a jealousy problem. She was partners with her ex-boyfriend and that bothered me. We used to fight about it all the time. Our relationship was still hanging in there despite the fighting about her partner. In Key West, I was more adventurous than her. It was like she had agoraphobia, and I did not know how to deal with it.

Once back in New Hope, I seemed to have a talent for getting publicity, I became nationally known, and had been on TV a few times. I had done a giant political painting. It was during the Mapplethorpe controversy. Robert Mapplethorpe was a gay photographer. Some of his pictures were flowers and some were photos of whips coming out of assholes. He got a show at a big museum in Washington D.C. I think it was the Corcoran Museum. The Museum got money from the National Endowment for the Arts. Jesse Helms, a conservative Senator from South Carolina, introduced a bill in Congress to ban money that went to obscene art. It went national.

I did an eighteen-by-twenty-four-foot painting of Adam and Eve, based on a painting by Titian. Twenty-four feet is two stories high. I placed it behind my art gallery. It was visible from a bridge in the center of New Hope. Tourist and locals alike watched me paint it. I used my face for Adam and my wife's face for Eve. On the serpent's face was a picture of Jesse Helms. I was the subject of a TV news show. It was hosted by Stephanie Stahl, a famous newscaster from Philadelphia. Other stations followed suit. Before you knew it, a wire service picked it up and I was on the front page of newspapers all over the country. It was called Adam and Eve without the fig leaf. It's something you would see in Europe, even at the Vatican. However, Jesse Helms' bill said any nudity is considered obscene.

One night I was listening to Saturday Night Live, and I heard a comedian tell a joke about it. Then I got some calls saying Oprah Winfrey had read an article about me and this project, and proceeded to do a show on art and censorship.

Another call was a death threat. This guy called late at night. He sounded drunk. He was asking some questions that sounded like threats. I hung up on him. This has nothing to do with Paris. I would still get these weird calls.

MURAL COMMISSION

I was getting a lot of mural commissions. I was working for some famous people and was serious about selling my art. I wanted a perfect relationship with my beautiful classy cosmopolitan wife, but I could not get over my jealousy about her business partner.

I went to London and worked for a month doing murals for the crowned Prince of Abu Dhabi. I got this job through a guy I studied marbleizing and wood graining with. He was an internationally known Trompe L'Oeil painter who was from London. I took his course in New York City. We became friends and he bought a painting from me. I was then able to do another course with him.

When he invited me to do this big job in London, I stayed two months. I went out a few times to a place called The World Ends, which was in a section of London called Camden Town. I met a beautiful Irish girl at that bar. I cheated several times on my wife when I was there. When I got back, I had an affair with a single woman who was large in the breasts and hips, and she got pregnant. She owned a successful restaurant. We lived in a small town and everyone knew about it. I humiliated my wife, so she had an affair with a social acquaintance of mine. I found them together and told her to move off the farm where we lived. Then we called the police on each other. It was a fiasco. After, she moved out and in with him. I got what I deserved. It was a low time in my life.

My Gallery was on Ney Alley in a tree house and it was about one hundred feet from where Artemisia moved in with her boyfriend. His apartment was on the second floor. He had a rifle and some other firearms up there. The day she moved in I was standing outside my gallery and I could see into their window from where I was standing. Next thing I hear this ping. What sounded like a .22 caliber bullet hit the

Memoirs of an Artist

dirt about ten feet in front of me. I had been shot at before – the 1968 riots, in 1975 with Steve on the way to the train station in Paris, and now Artemisia's boyfriend. We never got back together but remained close friends.

This was during the time I had an Art Gallery in New Hope on Mechanic Street. I was always painting in front of my gallery on Mechanic Street. All kinds of people would surround me and watch me paint.

It was around the time Chuck Barris came to town. It all started with a phone call on a Friday in the late afternoon. The phone rings, a man begins by saying hello and telling me it was Chuck. He says he has a job and was I interested? I said what kind of job. He says jobs like I used to do in Paris during my dark days. Someone needed to get taken care of. I said I am a flower child and artist and I don't do that. He says well what did you do in Paris? Chuck says people got hurt. I said if they did I did not mean it. I was trying to help the good guys. Then he says this job is different; some actors will be there and it is for a movie. Chuck asked me to ride around in a car with these actors and pretend we were going to do a hit. It was practice for a scene in a movie. I say how much? He says a couple of hundred. I say I could make more than that in my gallery. He sounds disappointed. The actors wanted to meet me. I said I was going to be in my gallery in New Hope the next day. They could come by and meet me. I knew Chuck had money. I figured I could sell him a painting. I told them to come at one o'clock.

The next day I was taking a nap on my couch in my gallery and at one o'clock I heard a knock on my door. These two guys came in. They seemed nervous because they had woken me up. I said that's okay. I think they were afraid about waking up a "dangerous" guy like me. I was afraid of five-year-old kids, because so many people had threatened to kill me. Chuck was not with them; it was an actor and a writer. They introduced themselves to me. The one guy's name was George Clooney. It was in the early 1990's and I had not heard of him. He said he was a star on daytime TV on some show about a hospital. I said where's Chuck? They said he dropped them off and went to run some errands. The other guy with George introduced himself as a writer.

Next George tells me he is doing a movie with Chuck called *Confessions of a Dangerous Mind* and they wanted me to help. The movie was about Chuck's experiences as a hit man. I said to George, what is it that you think I have done? George says that he was not there to judge me. The conversation turned to my wardrobe. George told me I was not dressed the way a political assassin was supposed to be dressed. I had on jeans that were two short with dried paint stains on them. I had on a ratty tee shirt with yesterday's lunch and today's breakfast on it. George was very smartly dressed, expensive loafers, very nicely pressed slacks and a beautiful Armani polo shirt. He looked like he had walked out of a GQ magazine fashion spread. George said I should dress more like my personality and more like my profession in Paris. George then asked me why I did what I did. I said I did it to avenge the wrongs done to the Jewish people especially during the Holocaust. He then said he was very proud of being an Italian but that did not mean he would go and kill for the Italian government.

The other guy who was with George was tall and had curly hair. He told me he was Jewish. I asked him if he could help the Jewish people. He said he didn't know. George seemed upset that I was not familiar with his TV show. He went on to say that he was getting more into movies, and phasing out of this doctor show.

We talked some more and I told them I no longer directly worked in espionage and that I was trying to make a go of it with my art. George then tells me only one of my paintings in my gallery showed signs of genius. He liked the others but this one long vertical painting hanging between two windows at one end of the room showed signs of genius. The painting was a landscape. It was a country road with trees on each side that created a canopied tunnel effect. There was light at the end of this tunnel. George liked that one. He said the art world was not a good place to live in if I was hiding. He said there was too much exposure in the art world and I could be found by people who may be looking for me. I said I was not hiding. He seemed to think my life could be in some sort of danger. I said radical PLO usually does not buy art. I was doing faux painting and murals in people's homes and I said it was unlikely that PLO sympathizers would hire me for a mural job. I said many of my clients were Jewish. George said again, well, maybe you would get a job with people that had something to do with the UN, and they would discover that you were a Mossad hit man. I said that was unlikely. They said Chuck wanted them to talk to me because I captured the craziness of that era. I said I was retired from that world and wanted to make it with my art. I wanted to become an art star. His friend, the tall writer with the curly hair, allowed me to do his portrait in black and white. He gave me twenty dollars.

Then later on that day I get this phone call. It was from a woman in Hollywood who said she was George Clooney's agent. She says I could make a great deal of money if I would help with the script. She then tells me to send her pictures of my art. I did and she called me back after she received them. She told me she wanted to buy one of my paintings sight unseen. I sent her the painting in Hollywood and she hung it in her house. We had several long conversations on the phone. I said to her, Can you help promote my paintings in Hollywood where she lived. She told me she could not tell people who I was because she said they would not believe her. She said people did like the painting and it reminded them of well-known Pennsylvanian impressionists.

About a week later I got a visit from a woman who was going to star in the movie with George Clooney. She said that Chuck told her to come see me. She said that Chuck said he wanted her to meet me as research for the movie that they were going to be in. She was wearing blue jeans with a red tank top. She had on sunglasses and was wearing sneakers on her feet. She had longish straight hair, nice eyes, and a nose that turned up a little on the end. She told me she had a brother she did not get along with. I told her I thought she was very beautiful. We talked about Paris and we talked about art. We talked about the American Impressionists in France. I told her my wife was from Florence, Italy. I told her that my wife owned a jewelry store in town and it was called Room at the Top. She told me she did a play with the name "Room at the Top" and that it was the hardest role she had ever done. She told me her name was Julia Roberts. She thought I was a hit man for the Mossad.

Chuck visited me several other times during that time period. One day he comes over unannounced to my gallery. Once again I had been sleeping on my couch. He wakes me up. I did not recognize him. He seemed angry about that because he was worth over one hundred million dollars because of his TV shows. He says you really don't recognize me? I said a lot of famous people come into my gallery, plus I was sleeping, and it takes me a while to wake up. He said I had the worst case of amnesia and post traumatic stress that he had ever seen. He said I would never become an art star until I got over my memory loss about Paris. He said I needed to embrace what happened to me in Paris so I would be a complete person. He said then my art would sell I would make more money and I would be famous.

He asked me to walk him out. Outside of my gallery, in the hallway on the second floor, there was an alcove. He stepped back into it. He beckoned me to join him in the alcove. I sensed he wanted to strangle me there. He had a bizarre look on his face. I also noticed he was wearing these boots with spike heels for men. People wore these in order to look taller. He told me again, embrace your past, then I would be whole and a success. He then told me if I were ever to write a book and mention his name he would have me killed. He said I could write a book about him in the year 2030.

One day he comes to my gallery again. He tells me sometime soon he will be bringing an attractive woman from Beverly Hills to meet me. He says this will be my big chance and I better not blow it. I said how was I supposed to act. He said just be yourself. A few weeks later, on a Saturday, I was painting plein air on the street in front of my gallery. He shows up with two women and then splits. One was very attractive and we got involved in a very nice somewhat intimate conversation. She looked a little disheveled, and had been drinking but was not drunk She had very white skin and red hair. She was into metaphysics and had written a book about reincarnation. She was also an actress in the movie business. She had a brother named Warren who was also an actor. Chuck was trying to put the two of us together. He was acting as a matchmaker. Her friend, who was her age, was also from Beverly Hills and she was with Shirley McClain on the trip as a companion. Chuck had been trying to get her to come out from the West Coast. And she finally agreed.

Shirley excused herself and went to the Ladies room. Her friend told me that Chuck wanted to introduce us because he thought we had a lot in common. Shirley comes back from the ladies' room and I try to go into high gear. I tell her, Yes I worked on operations with the Mossad in Paris. It was the first time I ever admitted it to anyone because I was attracted to her. I said, Yes that happened, but I was really a flower child, mystic at heart. I told her that I was going to write a book about my experiences seeing an alien named Pazuzu.

I talked about when I first met Avner in the Louvre and my experience with an inter-dimensional being. We talked about me going there for a visit and what we would do. She said I was pretty out there, having both an experience with my inter-dimensional friend Pazuzu and then being a bag man for the Mossad. She said I was not calmed down yet to write a book, but I had a lot of good stories I could draw on. I told her I was thinking about moving to the West Coast. She told me I could get mixed up with some bad characters out there if word got around about my dark past. She said I could end up being used by some wannabe writer. She told me I was better off staying in New Hope where everyone accepted me. We talked about substance abuse. I told her it's too bad she drank so much because she had such beautiful skin. There are other things we talked about that I am not going to mention.

I was getting a lot of newspaper coverage as well

as television spots on my projects. I was obsessed with having contacts with people in the press as a way to protect myself from the Mossad. I found that it helped me reach wider audiences. I was painting some sets at the local television station, as well as doing some sets for the Bucks County Playhouse. I was keeping myself truly busy in order to avoid the Mossad who were always right behind me.

One day my wife and son and I were shopping on Madison Avenue in New York City. We were outside a door looking in at a window. There was another person outside the store who looked like the owner. All of a sudden I hear a ping like a pebble hitting the wall. The man next to us seemed started and very nervous, like it was a gun shot. I just ignored it thinking what next.

A year and one half later in New Hope somebody said they were from law enforcement and approaches me. He said I should keep a file. He said someone was released from prison who took a shot at me a year and one half ago. He said the young man had emotional problems and was obsessed with my story and was very jealous. He had a uncle in Mossad. He only did a year and one half and had family connections.

Around this time, I found out about a three-month course at a place called the New York Film Academy in Manhattan. You would learn the fundamentals about writing, directing and editing your own movies. I signed on, commuting to New York City for the classes. There were a lot of hot chicks who were taking the course. There was a really pretty Japanese girl who I thought I was going to have a fling with. It fell apart at the last minute because I was helping her with her three-minute movie and something happened. She had her sixteen-millimeter camera set up in front of a storefront. I was helping her and she asked me if the reflection of the camera would show on the glass of the storefront she was shooting into. I told her I thought the reflection of the camera would not show in the glass and it did and she stopped talking to me.

My final project was a thirty-minute documentary called *An Artist and His Work*. It was about me. I interviewed two ex-wives, my father, my son, and a girlfriend to tell my story about my art. I managed to get it aired all over New Jersey, New York, and Pennsylvania. It helped my sales of paintings because I was meeting new people. I liked the process so much that I started making other documentaries in my free time.

I applied for a grant for a new project and was awarded a grant in my category – Art and Education. It was called *The New Hope Story*. It was about all the important artists that settled in the New Hope area in the turn of this Century. I had received the highest grant award that year; it was for ten thousand dollars. PBS bought it and aired it in the New York/Philadelphia area. My success in that arena, I felt, brought me additional places to hide from my sordid past.

I was still hanging around New Hope a lot. My close friend owned a restaurant called Karla's. He commissioned me to do a mural on the outside of his restaurant. I use to go there at night to socialize. One night a woman my age, with a European accent, came in looking for me. When someone pointed me out, she introduced herself. She said she was a friend of Gideon's and he thought we should meet. She was a survivor of Operation Wrath of God. I did not know exactly what she did. I suspected. She was not sure what I did but she knew it was something. She never been to the States. She had her boyfriend from Israel with her; they were engaged. He went for a walk while

I talked to this woman whose name was Jen. She had a hard time like Yael. Her involvement was her whole life now, even though it happened some years ago. I mean after the Munich Olympic incident, Operation Wrath of God went on for several years in different countries. Some innocent people had been killed. A lot of people were hurt. She witnessed a horrific killing that she never would recover from. My memories were still in that box that actually had a name; it was a form of amnesia. She sensed that after we talked a while. She said I was in for a rude awakening and she did not know how strong I was and if I would recover. I invited her and her boyfriend to my house where I had most of my art. She declined. She had accomplished her goal, which was to see me, and she had seen enough. There were no ill feelings between us; she just said she had seen enough. I eventually had my epiphany and breakdown which she was talking about. It happened after the death of a friend. I was the one who found him. The sight of a dead body triggered something that opened that Pandora's Box.

November 4, 1995, Yitzak Rabin was assassinated in Israel by a rightwing fanatic. He opposed the Oslo peace accord. Rabin was the architect for what was known as the Peace of the Brave. He shook hands with Yassar Arafat at the White House. My time was measured by political events in Israel. Despite everything that happened between me and the Mossad, I was an ardent supporter of the State of Israel.

I was still living on the farm. I was working in my studio there. Someone knocked on my door. He was a man about my age. I invited him in and he told me some things. He said he worked for a famous writer. He said they wrote books about espionage. He said they were working on a series that was inspired by my experiences. He went on to say I was the most written about person in espionage and how did I feel about that. He said he may have some ideas about how I could profit from it. I had really conflicting emotions and a rage built up in me. There were people out there who knew more about me than I knew about myself. That pissed me off. I said I was honored. I said I wanted no fame when it came to espionage. I wanted to make it with my art. That was my priority. I did not want to be a famous spy that was an average artist. I wanted to be a great artist that at one time sidelined as a spy. I choose my art over fame and money. My art was gaining acceptance, but I was still more famous as a spy. I think Chuck Barris, who hung with espionage writers, had talked to them because he was so freaked out by my post-traumatic stress or inability to talk about Paris.

I was playing a lot of tennis at the time. My partner, a librarian from New Hope, invited me for doubles where I met a lady named Leslie. She was five-foot-nine, brunette, perfect figure, and was a woman with a big career. She was born on the border of Texas and Mexico. The closest airport was McAllen. She grew up about thirty-five miles from Padre Island. She learned how to rustle steers to the ground in the rodeo before she had her first period. She was a beauty queen in high school and college. She had been a famous county commissioner in Gettysburg, PA, where her husband was a professor. She ran for state senate, lost, but landed a job at the Department of Environmental Protection in PA under the Casey administration. She then divorced. Although a democrat, she got the job as Commissioner for Clean Air under Christy Whitman, governor of New Jersey.

That's when I met her. She was new to the area. We played a decent game of tennis together and before you know it we moved in together on the farm.

She worked and I painted at my gallery in New Hope. I think she looked like Jane Fonda. After sixth months we got married. She had two grown sons from her first marriage. One was diagnosed with schizophrenia in college. He was in and out of the hospital.

A few weeks after we got married he committed suicide in Texas. She began drinking heavy and shortly afterwards moved back to Texas to open a clinic for disturbed young people. Actually, Leslie had a drinking problem when I first met her. Who am I to talk? I had a substance abuse problem too. I smoked weed all the time. Alcohol is different than weed. We used to fight about her drinking. To this day I do not like being around alcohol. I will never sell a painting to anyone who is drinking a lot.

Life went on. I was not getting any money from my family, so I had to keep working. Before the ink was even dry on the quickie divorce I met someone else. During this time, I began seeing a nurse with a Master's Degree in anesthesia. Her name was Hana. We met when she came into my art gallery studio with her girlfriend, Barbara, who was a mutual friend. We went canoeing in the Delaware that afternoon. I then invited her for dinner that night. We had a wonderful time. It was refreshing. She told me that night that I was a candidate to be her lover. She was drop-dead gorgeous and smart. Her personality was very cute. I called her pure Valley Girl. She made me wait a month before I got the action. It was the most painful month I ever spent because she started sleeping over right away. The pain was the blisters I had between my legs.

She had a pedigree address. The Waterworks, a converted factory on the Delaware River had been redesigned into luxury apartments. Anybody who lived there was in the "super in-crowd." A lot of celebs lived there too. She drove a big black Mercedes Benz.

She was born in Korea and was adopted by a college professor and his wife. They were also missionaries. She had brothers and sisters who were also adopted. She grew up outside of Penn State in central Pennsylvania.

She had a face like a beautiful Buddha. Hana was also well read and loved art. She had the look of an Asian Bohemian. She at first appeared to be demure, my kind of woman. Hana had never married nor had kids. Her only addiction was to work over one hundred hours a week. Her other flaw was her attraction to selfish men. I realized that the demure look was a façade but I still was deeply in love with her. In private and in public she liked to yell, scream, and rant. By then I was a filmmaker who was in newspapers, magazines, and in art periodicals. I also told no one that different writers and Hollywood celebrities had come and talked to me, to try to get me to help with their movies. I told none of my close friends in New Hope that Chuck Barris had come to visit me. A man who claimed to kill thirty people for the CIA.

Shortly after meeting, Hana and I moved in with each other. We were staying mostly at my place. It was on Mechanic Street, hub of the art world in New Hope. Our house was built in 1740. It had many leaks that had not been addressed since then. I had a shop in front and an apartment with a courtyard in back. My son Rembrandt was also with us. Not only was the house old, it had ghosts and was on the ghost tour.

One night a fire started in another unit and woke us up. We were awakened by the familiar sounds of explosions, like popping light bulbs. I was the first to awaken; after all I was a bomb maker and hit man. Before waking up I had been dreaming of an apparition of a woman in a revolutionary war outfit. The fire soon spread to my gallery and apartment, causing upheaval in our life. To cleanse, after my fire, we planned a trip to Key West, Florida. When it rains it pours. Besides planning the trip to Key West we also made a month-long quickie trip to Brazil and Carnival.

BRAZIL

Hana met these two lesbian tour guides who were from Brazil. They were both beautiful fashion models. We signed up for their tour. One other lady from the area signed up too. It was four women and me. Nobody was fat but that was okay. We flew to Rio. We arrived three weeks before Carnival.

CARNIVAL GIRLS

Billy Selesnick

We stayed in Le Blanc on the beach next to the Copa Cabana section and also next to Ipanema, made famous by the Jose Feliciano song, "The Girl from Impanema." That was the artist neighborhood. The beaches there were the finest in the world. The waves were huge.

Rio was different than the States. The States were puritanical compared to Brazil. Old men walked around in bikini bathing suits on busy shopping streets with young women dressed like hookers about to go for a swim. The beaches there were segregated. One beach was for European nudists and Brazilian artists and fashion models. No fat women in Brazil, at least in Rio. The next beach was for middle class Brazilian families. One beach was for surfers. The beach closest to the mountains outcropping was for street gangs. That was the first beach where I did a plein air painting. They all came over to talk to me. Cocaine was real cheap in Rio. The kids all wanted to make friends with me. There were no hang-ups about race there. There was total race mixing. It was Brazilian Indians inter marrying with descendants of black slaves and the Portuguese white settlers. The beaches were the best I have ever seen.

So then we go to a town called Paraty. Paraty is a preserved port and colonial town with a population of thirty-six thousand, that runs along the coastline of the state of Rio de Janeiro. Paraty had become a popular tourist destination. The town is located in the bay of Iha Grande, on the Costa Verde coast, a lush green corridor in the state of Rio de Janeiro. It was a five-hour drive from Rio. It is dotted with many tropical islands rising up as high as 1300 meters. Behind the town are tropical forests, mountains and waterfalls. Paraty is surrounded by many parks and nature preserves. The municipality is close to indigenous villages, and Afro-Brazilian Qquilones. In1667 it was founded by Portuguese colonists in a region populated only by Indians. After the discovery of the world's richest gold mines in 1696, the mountains of Paraty became an export center for the gold to Rio and then on to Portugal. That led to the building of the gold trail. The gold trail was constantly under attack from pirates and thieves.

We stayed in an old colonial villa made into a hotel. There was a pool in the center in a courtyard. The rooms surrounded it. The owner was a retired Brazilian movie star. She had come to America to play opposite Ricky Riccardo, Lucille Ball's husband. She made many movies and retired in Paraty to open her hotel. It was an international hot spot. People came from all over the world to stay there.

She saw me painting by the pool. We were smitten with each other. She bought a small painting from me. Many times that is the beginning of an affair. She invited me to a suite at the hotel. She had the face and body of a famous actress. Who cared that she was not fat. She removed her dentures and the rest was history.

I finally did get to see some rotund women in Brazil. It was after we left Paraty and we went to visit some Indian tribes. It was deep in the rain forest. This tribe had little contact with white people. They went without shirts, both men and women. The men carried spears. The women carried their children and grandchildren. It was there that I saw some robust women. They could have posed for a picture in *National Geographic*. We toured the rest of the country, seeing many things.

After a few weeks we returned to Rio for carnival. There are many celebrations around the time of carnival. There are parties and balls for two to three weeks before the start of Carnival.

That night we had tickets to one of the balls that was opening the week of carnival. There were different balls around Rio each night. There was a gay ball on Monday, a family ball on Tues, etc. etc. The ball we were going to was the gangster and poor people's ball. The only requirements were you had to wear red and black. We went to this ball. I. I thought it was déjà vu. We all got felt up until we got to our table. We just dealt with it. It was really crowded and there were cops all over the place. Everybody was smoking dope and snorting drugs. The Brazilian disco music was so loud you could not even think. We all had a good time. We still had a few days before the big parade which was the climax of Carnival.

The next day we were walking around our neighborhood. On each street there were drum circles going on at different outside cafes. It was like everyone was off work and on each street there was an all night and day party. We go by this one café where there had been a twenty-four-hour drum circle going on for a few days. We stop and watch. The people playing the drums looked like they had been high on mushrooms for days. There was a crowd of male and female dancers scantily dressed. Many were practically nude wearing a thong, barefoot, beads, and feathers reminiscent of Indians from the Amazon. Some had their faces and bodies painted. People were communicating telepathically because people were from all over the world. We decided to hang out and have a drink. The drink mixture was made from bark, roots and ingredient them came from the jungle. A Shaman from the Amazon had brought it. This Shaman although he lived deep in the jungle far from civilization had journeyed to Rio for carnival. He looked exactly like a Shaman was supposed to look like.

People in Rio during carnival wear costumes like our American Halloween. This Shaman even had his spear.

We found some chairs close to the drums. We sipped our drinks, maybe ten minutes later I began to feel really strange, it was like time had slowed down and everything was going in slow motion. Then I felt as if I was outside of my body. I went out through the top of my head. It was a sensation that I was familiar with. The drums were really loud and I was in tune with the sound waves. The frequency was such that it felt like a time warp into another dimension. So I was above my body floating in conjunction with the drumbeat. I had been there before at drum circles in Woodstock. This though was intensified by the drink, which was a mixture known to cause hallucinations. Several nights later was the final night of Carnival. It was held at a parade ground in the suburbs. We had expensive seats in a box on the front row. The girls had joined a samba club and were participants in one part of the parade. I was in the box by myself. My job was to get pictures of them when they went by. I completed my assignment and they came back down to watch the rest of the parade. We left Brazil the next day.

When we arrived back in New Hope I began to paint pictures inspired by my trip to Brazil. They were of scantily dressed young women covered in feathers and dancing as in some sort of trance I did dozens of canvases inspired by the culture of Brazil. Shortly afterwards we moved to Key West.

Chapter Nine

BILLY'S PAINTING OF SLOPPY JOES

Key West is in Monroe County. It is also the county seat. It is the southernmost city in America. Key West is 129 miles southwest of Miami. In pre-Columbia time Key West was inhabited by the Caloosa people. Another group of Indians that settled afterwards were taken to Cuba by the early Spanish conquerors where they died out.

The first European to arrive was Ponce De Leon in 1521. As Florida became a Spanish territory, a fishing village was established. It had a small garrison there. In between, it had a thriving salvage business and a sponge business. It was also famous for its cigar factories. There was a salt industry there in the 1830s. Early settlers off Key West and Duck Key manufactured sea salt using natural salt pond basins on both islands. Salt was essential for preserving food in those days because there was no refrigeration. Key West is a place famous for its Key Lime Pies. They are exported all over the world.

Key West was used to fight off pirates and buccaneers when the United States gained possession of Florida and the Florida Keys in 1821. The island of Key West took on an importance as a naval base. Key West became a safe base of operation to fight piracy that was ravaging the trading vessels traveling through the Gulf Stream superhighways, heading to the Gulf of Mexico going toward New Orleans.

Key West was incorporated in 1828. Within ten years, it was the largest and wealthiest city in the territory of Florida. It could only be reached by ship. This was a fact of life that continued until Henry Flagler's Florida East Coast Railroad extension was finished in 1912. It was the very isolating thing that kept Key West from the rest of the world that contributed to its wealth.

KEY WEST SUNSET

Homesteading the keys, Bahamians also homesteaded other keys in the early 19th Century. Settling in small family groups to farm the thin soil they were familiar with cultivating the unique land of limestone islands. The Bahamians worked at farming pineapples and key limes.

Key West is also famous for Florida lobsters. I like them just as much as Maine lobsters. There is a big Lobster Festival in the summer during lobster season.

Key West is also famous for what's called Key West Pinks, a really tender variety of shrimp. There were a number of whorehouses in Key West. They're still there fronting as strip clubs. Meyer Lansky had a home in Key West. That was when he had gambling interests in Cuba.

THE STRAND

Memoirs of an Artist

Key West is only ninety miles to Cuba. It also had a number of military and navy bases and military related businesses. There are a number of hotels, motels, guesthouses where clothing is optional, resorts, gay guesthouses and a few trailer parks. Key West has been a major tourist destination since visited by Ponce de Leon.

Most of the nice trailer parks are on Stock Island. That is the next key going north. At one time, Key West had a lot of poor. Many have moved to Stock Island as Key West has become gentrified.

Ernest Hemmingway had a house in Key West starting in the 1930s. His house is now a museum. It was the first house in Key West with a swimming pool. Tennessee Williams also lived there. It has long been a haven for writers and artists.

In the 1960s a lot of hippies and flower children and artists began arriving, starting these sunset festivals at Mallory Square. At sunset, entertainers, artists, actors, pirates. drug dealers. drug addicts, dogs, cats, bears, vendors of ice cream, conch fritters and lemonade, fire dancers, people who walked on hot coals (me), the whole nine yards would meet there. The average yearly temperature there is 87 degrees.

Key West, in American folklore, was considered one of the most wayout places on the planet. It is also directly located in Hurricane Alley. More hurricanes hit this island than I care to remember. Did you know that a study was done that found that birth rates rise nine months after a hurricane. True fact. Everybody sees it on TV. People party during hurricanes.

I forgot to mention that it is on the edge of the Bermuda Triangle. There are more shipwrecks with Spanish gold than I could recount here. There have been a record number of alien space craft sightings.

KEY WEST HOUSE

Hana and I looked into investment properties and we found one with a transient license. That meant, when we were not there our unit could be rented by the night. It was managed by a company and our unit, which we named the Artist House, actually made a profit.

KEY WEST HOUSE OIL ON CANVAS

I had renovated it to look like an artist studio. I did murals there, I hung up my paintings. I put in a big easel. I did faux painting all over the unit. When we sold it we more than doubled our money in two years.

Right around 9\11 we moved full time to Key West. I don't think I went to my box of secrets much then, but once or twice someone, a stranger, would approach me and start talking about Munich. They would mention they had tracked me down and/or paid money for the information of my whereabouts. I had a kind of amnesia about that. At this point in my life, aside from being occasionally reminded, I would go long periods without thinking about Paris.

I always apply my lessons of being an espionage agent wherever I go. This place was a paradise of wheeling and dealing. Key West is a snake pit of famous criminals and felons. I felt right at home and began making money on the side. Immediately I found the best weed dealers. You want to know how many people came to me and wanted weed. Well, it was enough. I ate in fancy restaurants every night, with an entourage no less. I liked hanging out with the homeless and people that were like me – mentally impaired.

The CIA had a listening post to keep an eye on Fidel. The post has a huge antenna at one of the beaches. I did a painting of that round antenna and in some countries that could land you in jail, maybe never seeing the light of day again. You would not believe who bought that painting.

Large suitcases of one-dollar bills were a trademark of mine. That's how I would get paid for a lot of paintings. I got to the point where I was gluing them to paintings and using them as backgrounds.

Key West was also home to some super right-wingers, Bay of Pigs kind of stuff. I told no one there of my past. I kept my mouth shut and made a little on the side.

This was a productive time for my art. I probably did over one hundred paintings a year during the time that I lived there.

I was able to sell most of them to tourists and locals. I did shows at different galleries and restaurants.

BOAT OIL ON CANVAS

I also sold my work when I painted plein air at different locations around town. I also displayed my paintings on the porch of my house. I had a gallery in my house then.

I took any commission I could get. Some guy who owned a bar up north commissioned me to do a painting. He wanted it for his bar. They served a lot of barbecue. Anyway he paid me to do a painting of two pigs fucking. I also did murals around town.

There are a lot of other artists my age, actually all ages, that did exactly what I did. Some made more money, some less. It all depended on your hustle. I added tap dancing to my street show and that added a few dollars in my bucket I had put out for tips. I also had postcards made of my art, so I had items starting at a dollar.

BOAT OIL ON BOARD

Key West was a place where Cuban refugees would wash up on shore in rafts and other homemade boats. It was not unusual to be at the beach and spot these people seeking freedom from Fidel. I no longer have an infatuation with communist Cuba. I have friends on both sides of the issue.

I would like to visit Cuba as a tourist and see what it is like. Now that the old regime is loosening its grip, perhaps I will.

A lot of my Cuban friends would never go back there and are very militant about it. It's a hot issue in Key West and South Florida.

In 1982, on April 23, Key West attempted succession from the union of the United States. This happened after the United States border patrol established roadblocks at the end of the mainland to screen for drugs and illegal aliens. This affected the local tourist industry. Independent Key West rebelled and created its own flag and tried to establish an independent homeland. You could even get your own Conch Republic passport. Every year there is a ten-day commemoration celebration. A battle between the US Coast Guard boats and the Conch Republic boats takes place in the waters off Mallory Square. It ends up being a mock water fight.

Every year around Halloween there is a two-week event that takes place called Fantasy Fest. It culminates on Halloween with a famous and large parade that rivals New Orleans' Mardi Gras and Carnival in Rio de Janeiro. The parade in Key West is known for its outrageous costumes and nudity. Artists set up on the street there with body painting spray booths. Customers get naked and have their bodies spray painted in different costumes. Many will be leopard skin women or zebra stripes. Maybe an artist will spray paint a tux on you. You could be spray painted as a nurse or butler. Most of the spray-painted costumes are sexual. This parade starts around sunset and stops at sunrise. The floats are a sight to behold and many hours go into their preparation.

I have seen all kinds of things on Halloween night. One guy was standing by his convertible while his wife lay in the back seat naked on her back. The husband was outside the car pimping his wife and collecting the money.

The two weeks of the festival before the Halloween blowout has different events. It could be a dog parade one night or a Bahamian parade with dancing on another. Different events, different parts of town. There could be a pirate night.

My relationship with Hana was rocky. She did not like the fact that I smoked weed and kept the house messy. We were also partners in a business venture where we bought investment properties, renovated them, and then rented them out.

Most of our properties were next door to each other, and at one time we owned half the houses on our street.

Every homeless guy and gal in Key West knew I was an easy mark. They hung around our house all the time. They knew that I would give them part time jobs and they could buy alcohol. I was not a big hit with a lot of the neighbors or Hana.

It was the heyday of the real estate boom. I was able to brag that I was a self-made millionaire due to the high rate of value during the housing boom. For so many years I had struggled with money – eating out of the garbage, working on garbage trucks, working for the Mossad, dealing weed. I finally had financial security. I was a millionaire. I had been a starving artist my whole life. I was finally an equal to my father.

I bought the best weed in town. I spent six hundred an ounce and smoked an ounce a week. That was another sore point between Hana and me. She did not like me bragging that I was a self-made millionaire.

Hana worked in Miami; she was a nurse anesthetist. She was an RN with a Masters Degree in anesthesia. When she would come down on weekends, we would go for long walks, and fix up the houses. I had been a cheat my whole life when it came to other women. I loved Hana and never cheated on her. I also liked it that everywhere we went people thought I was with Yoko Ono.

In 2004 I began to experience numbness in my pinky on my right hand. Shortly thereafter, I had pain when opening and closing my fingers. Then the pain extended to my elbow. This meant I could not paint. Mister 007 can't paint, what's a guy to do?

Some days the pain was so severe I could not walk. It seemed that my arm weighed five hundred pounds. It felt like my foot had fallen asleep and had a lot of numbness but it was in my arm. I walked to the grocery store but was taken home in a grocery cart. I went to my family doctor and he did an electrocardiogram. My heart was normal. He sent me to several specialists.

In Key West nobody feels sorry for you. That's because it's the homeless capital of the world. There was homeless living in wheel chairs on the street. Who is going to feel sorry for me?

After going to several doctors I was diagnosed with neuropathy of my arm and hand. I was being treated with different drugs that changed my personality. I began to develop a dependency to painkillers. I was scaring my friends. I was acting in a way that was not congruent with my normally mellow personality. I was not myself.

I chose to have surgery. I had an ulnar nerve transdisposition on my elbow and at the same time, carpal tunnel surgery on my hand. Within a few days a serious infection set in, and I was readmitted to the hospital where I developed a bad case of Mersa. It was then I developed an addiction to morphine through intravenous injections, the "pump."

After my release from the hospital I continued to have a problem with painkillers and developed a bout of mania. Having mania meant no sleeping for days or weeks on end. Then I had an entourage around the clock to order around. I had this entourage because I could not cook or even wipe my ass because of the surgery on my hand. I could use my left hand but I found it hard to have the use of one hand. It meant I burned through fifty thousand bucks in two months. I had gotten a home equity loan.

A year before I had started to develop a passion

for making movies again. I worked a year on a documentary called *The End of the Road*. Most of it took place in a hurricane. That was the summer that we had some twenty storms. It was the year of Wilma, Katrina and numerous others. I never left the island once during those storms.

One night I thought the wind was going to blow in the windows I had refused to board up. I boarded them for all the other storms and nothing had happened. All that happened was I broke a few toes when I was boarding up because big sheets of heavy wood would slip and fall on my feet. Anyway, the night that the window blew in was the night I stepped on my glasses and broke them in the dark. Then this huge tree in front of our house blew over. A four-foot by ten-foot piece of sidewalk was raised vertically in the air. We lost power for weeks. The toilet stunk, we were hot and sweaty, and the water was bad. I was out shooting a movie while all this was going on. I turned my truck into a film production vehicle and art gallery. I ran a clothes line on the outside of the truck with my dirty underwear on it. I wrote on my underwear visit Selesnick Gallery.

I wrote it, directed, and also starred in it. It had a limited release and I sold a few copies and broke even on it. Some consider it a cult classic. The story was that there was a series of hurricanes and the Seven Mile Bridge was cut off. Many of the big wigs left, some on their private jets. The poor ones, the artists from Mallory Square, stayed. So did the homeless. Well, in my movie, that was loosely based on *King of Hearts*, the homeless and artists band together and take over the island.

The premise of the French film, *King of Hearts*, was that during World War I the people of a small town leave before the advancing army reaches it.

There is an insane asylum in town and they let themselves out and take the town over in advance of the arriving army. The story was told by me in a form of a mural that I painted throughout the movie. It was interspersed with archival and historical footage of the History of Key West.

At the end of the movie, my character was depressed and tries to swim to Cuba. When he drowns and his life goes before him, an alien named Pazuzu rescues him and takes him into outer space. Then my art becomes worth a lot of money.

Hana did not like the fact that I was putting so much time and money into the movie. She wanted me to focus on my paintings and save money. We had some arguments about it. She was making veiled threats about leaving me if I did not tow the line.

The next thing was Hana and I broke up. One Sunday night after she left for Miami I got this call from a woman. She asked me if I was Hana's boyfriend, I said yes. She said I am sorry to have to tell you this but your girlfriend is having an affair with my husband. They work together at the hospital. I was in shock. My unstable situation caused me to lose my house in foreclosure. I had gone through my money with the surgeries. I could not get any money out of my house because the housing bubble just burst.

Around this time, I got into minor trouble with the police. My next-door neighbor was watching me because I was behaving erratically.

I was walking on hot coals on the sidewalk in front of my house. I was practicing for a spot at sunset at Mallory Square. That's where artists and performers gather at sunset and panhandle. She saw me and called the police and they started watching me. Finally, one night she called the police because I was playing the piano too loud, and the police came over.

I had gotten a piano because I thought that by playing it and exercising my fingers, I would speed up the healing in my hand. My friend let them in. The detective asked if there was weed in the house. He said if I admitted that I had some he would go easy on me. I showed him where it was and even though I was handcuffed and brought downtown, I was let out an hour later and not taken to jail.

I got a summons for a misdemeanor, under a half-ounce of weed. I appeared in court and my sentence was a court appointed session with a psychologist, who administered a test to see if I needed substance abuse counseling. I took the test and failed. I had to do six court-ordered sessions with him.

My father came to visit and did an intervention. He offered to set me up in Palm Beach County if I left the Keys and walked away from my house. My house was really underwater. It was a dark period. I had tremendous guilt. Without saying goodbye to my friends, I decided to leave Key West for Palm Beach Gardens.

I begged Hana to give me another chance but she wouldn't. She did remain my friend and tried to help me put my life back together. I was however taking medications prescribed by my doctor that were causing problems. Then there was another incident. I was lonely because Hana had left me. I would walk by this lap dance parlor every day when I went to the grocery store. I was feeling really lonely one day and decided to go in. I got a lap dance by a lady named Robin. I thought she was really nice. She also did lap dances at your house for more money. She came over to do a lap dance and I preferred that ambiance to the lap dancers' office next to the grocery store. She came over several times. During the day I started hanging around where she worked, next to the grocery store, and I was making a pest of myself. The management finally kicked me out and I was no longer allowed to get lap dancers or have Robin come over for private ones.

One night a friend named Larry was visiting and I wanted to see Robin. Larry calls up the lap dancing place and said he wanted a private lap dance but uses the address next door to me because I no longer was allowed to do business there. Larry asked for Robin but they sent another girl. When the girl arrived at the house next to mine Larry had already left. I told the girl I wanted to find out how Robin was doing. She came in and I got a lap dance. When it was time for her to leave I paid her and she owed me change. I was waiting for my change and she did not want to give it to me. I was standing in front of the door and she wanted to leave. She still refused to give me my change so I stood in front of the door.

She finally called her office. It was real close by so the management, along with Robin, arrived minutes later. A big yelling match had ensued and someone called the police.

The policeman was trying to get everyone's version of what happened and I was yelling and screaming. I was sure the police would be on my side – after all, I was a homeowner and they were lap dancers and pimps. The policeman sided with them. I was lead away in handcuffs, taken to jail and booked for felony kidnapping because I had stood in front of the door and would not let her leave.

I was taken to jail and put in a cell with a teenage guy who had been arrested for crack. He was driving and the cops stopped him. Before he was stopped he ate all his crack. He was spinning around and really hyper confined in that cell. He got out the next day. So did I. In all my life I had never been arrested. For

Memoirs of an Artist

all my weed dealing and involvement with the Mossad, I had never been arrested. I had to go before a judge the next morning. He let me out on ten thousand dollars bail. It never went to court and the charges were dropped. The girl from the strip club and their management did not show up at the court date.

My father came to visit and did an intervention. He offered to set me up in Palm Beach County if I left the Keys and walked away from my house. My house was really underwater. It was a dark period. I had tremendous guilt. Without saying goodbye to my friends, I decided to leave Key West for Palm Beach Gardens.

Chapter Ten

I moved to a place called East Pointe in Palm Beach Gardens; it was a gated community. I had a condo there, which was a few streets away from my parents. Palm Beach Gardens is nothing like the island of Palm Beach. It's reminiscent of a nice neighborhood in Connecticut but instead it's in Florida. There were a lot of rules; it was the exact opposite of Key West. If you walked to one of the pools, you had to wear a shirt. You had to have blinds on your windows and I could not lean any paintings on my windowsill. If you went to the clubhouse for dinner you had to wear certain attire. No motorcycles or trucks after six. No dogs over six pounds. It was not really my kind of place. The women all have jobs and there are not a lot of artists who live in the Gardens. It's pleasant but boring. There was a gym which offered yoga classes and a few dozen tennis courts and hot tubs.

There are many ponds and lakes on the property. There were many sand hill cranes that lived on the two golf courses. There were a lot of birds.

One morning I saw a wild bobcat. Also there was an alligator in one of the lakes. Rehabilitation from my surgery was long and painful. I did yoga everyday for two years at the Ultima Gym in West Palm. I also did physical therapy for a year. I began painting and was having a hard time finding a new market during the economic recession.

After breaking up with Hana, I began meeting women online. I had many dates but few affairs. Hana and I remained friends and hopefully will for the remainder of my life. She has come through for me during some difficult times.

Memoirs of an Artist

    I drove all over Florida painting lighthouses using Palm Beach County as my base. There are twenty-eight Lighthouses in Florida and eventually I painted all of them. I actually started the series when I was in Key West. I painted the Key West Lighthouse at least a dozen times. It was directly across the street from the Hemingway House. There were other artists who would set up in that area and it was competitive. The police would come by and tell the artists painting outside that they could not paint there. I also did a lot of paintings of the Hemingway House.

    When I moved to Palm Beach County I first painted the Jupiter Lighthouse. Then went south to Fort Lauderdale and did Hillsborough from several different angles. I went there and painted plein air. I also took photographs and would work on them at home. I sold one on the spot there.

    Then I painted Cape Florida on the tip of Key Biscayne. I painted that one on the beach when I was out on a date. There is a story associated with that lighthouse. It's the oldest lighthouse in Florida. It was first built in 1825. The lighthouse had been damaged several times throughout its history, from Seminole Indian attacks, pirates, Civil War battles, and hurricanes.

    Another day, I went to Coconut Grove in Miami and hired a boat to take me to Fowley Rocks. We went by Stiltsville which were houses in the middle of the ocean built on stilts. When we got to Fowey Rocks, which was about an hour's boat ride I took pictures at sunset. I later painted it a few times in my studio.

    The island of Palm Beach has a year-round population of 10,648 and seasonal population of thirty thousand. Palm Beach was established as a resort by Henry Morrison Flagler, founder of Standard Oil. He also was responsible for bringing the railroad all the way to Key West. His mansion in Palm Beach is now a museum called White Hall. It's right across the street from The Breakers, a famous hotel that he built.

My second wife's grandfather had a big mansion there called The Warden House. He was a big stockholder in Standard Oil.

Palm Beach has a lot of incredible subject matter. One of my favorite artists is Maxfield Parrish. He was inspired by Palm Beach's beautiful subject matter. You see a lot of plein air painters working around town. You meet interesting international people and the beaches are beautiful. Parking is probably the most expensive beach parking in the world. Also there are no public bathrooms.

There are really fun nightclubs and a lot of women that get work done on their faces and bodies.

In 1981 an organization was established to preserve the architecture of Mizner, Wyeth, Fatio, and Volk. I especially liked painting buildings designed by Mizner. I painted a number of his buildings.

I tried living on the island of Palm Beach during this time. I painted plein air and sold all of my paintings. I lived on Oleander Street. I also painted a lot of bougainvillea and there are plenty there. I painted those red roofs with the curved tiles. You see a lot of that in Paris. So really the subject matter is very European and that inspired me.

It really was not my style socially because the island has a reputation for being snobby, so it's a hard place to make friends, but the subject matter there is really nice and I liked Worth Avenue and the small shops on the Vias, the alleyways off the Avenue. I would go out to clubs in Palm Beach and dated many women. The club scene is amusing and the Leopard Lounge at the Chesterfield is a hoot. That's a place where older women go to meet younger men. The ceiling there is an erotic mural painted by some famous Italian artist.

There is also another

PALM BEACH OIL ON CANVAS

where older women go to meet younger men. The ceiling there is an erotic mural painted by some famous Italian artist.

There is also another profession that is right up my alley. It's called being a walker. That means an older widow hires you to walk the dog. Then you change light bulbs. Then you take the garbage out. Then you get the car keys and pick up dry-cleaning and groceries. At dinner parties you start out parking cars, and then you may help serve in the kitchen. If you are good, you may end up painting the house and mowing the lawn. Maybe at some point you will be paying the bills for her and signing the checks. Then you start wheeling your employee around in a wheelchair. Then if things work out you get the guesthouse on top of the garage.

If you are lucky, the woman you work for has a house on the beach. If you clean up nice and have nice teeth, you will end up being a paid escort. One charity event you may be taking her to is at Mar-a-Lago, the resort and exclusive club owned by Donald Trump. That is on South Ocean Drive. It is at the end of the southernmost bridge into Palm Beach.

Or you could be escorting your client to the Society of the Four Arts on the main road coming into town. It's the street with the tall palm trees and all the banks are on both sides of the street, Royal Palm Way. Many men made their bones in Palm Beach doing just that, being a walker. The majority of them are gay but not all.

When I did live on the island I did walk a dog or two but it never went anywhere. I dated a few wealthy widows and some poor ones too with dentures.

Every time I rent a tux I look like a headwaiter. I have had a small dog for twelve years. She is half Pomeranian and half Chihuahua. She is eight pounds and she has introduced me to many clients and wealthy widows with small dogs. Her name is Shelby and she bites new people and new dogs the first time she meets them.

One couple who I knew from New Hope had a mansion on the island. I gave them a price for a mural on the outside of their house. There are incredible outdoor murals painted on some of the houses there.

There is also a lucrative profession for women in South Florida. It's called being a "nurse" to an older man who is vulnerable, lonely, and rich. One called the Black Widow did time in Martin County jail. The newspaper said she took care of an older man's checkbook. She then took one hundred and seventy-five thousand to put down on a house. She used to come into my gallery that I later opened in Port Salerno in Martin County, which is 40 miles north of Palm Beach. She was going to buy one of my paintings that had a twenty-four carat gold background.

Against the backdrop of people struggling to survive I would find solace in my painting. My paintings were realistic with a lot of detail and they took hours of concentration to manifest. While I painted I would go into a trance state. While there I would communicate with the Masters from different eras. They would offer me tips on how to paint. This trance state was different then the trance state that drums would take me. The drum trance was like what happened in the Old Testament when The Hebrew people brought down the walls of Jericho, through sound waves. The trance state through painting took me to a conversation with a deceased artist. With the drum trance I would leave my body, with the painting trance I would be painting and the spirit of the artist I was talking to would envelop me.

Over the years when people would see me when I was painting they would say, you look like you just woke up from a nap. When I would paint I would channel my favorite artists. Palm Beach Gardens was not really my thing. I decided to take a trip to New Orleans because I had always heard that it was art friendly and there was a big art community at Jackson Square. A portrait artist I knew from Paris was living and working there.

New Orleans is a port and the largest city in Louisiana. It is named after the Duke of Orleans who was Regent for Louis XV from 1715 to 1723. New Orleans is influenced by European culture and was established by French colonists. New Orleans is famous for its food and music. It is known as the birthplace of jazz. New Orleans also has many festivals. Its most well-know festival is Mardi Gras which dates back to Colonial times. Jackson Square is in the center of the French Quarter. Its layout was based on seventeenth-century Place des Vosges in Paris. It is the size of a city block. In the center stands a life size equestrian statue of Andrew Jackson. On the north side of the square stands the Saint Louis Cathedral and is a famous landmark. In 1920 it became a gathering place for painters.

    I was driving there with a woman. She was very tall. I met her on line on a dating website. She was a sculptress and her name was Fifi. She had a sixty-year old parrot who was coming with us on the trip. We had been dating a while and she had come with me on some lighthouse trips. She lived on the island of Palm Beach and we got along, and we split expenses. I was not happy in Palm Beach Gardens and was looking for a new place to live. We made the twelve-hour car ride and checked into this Bed and Breakfast that was on the edge of the French Quarter. My first impression was that it looked like a decaying mansion. It smelled like mildew and that everything was rotting. Little did we know that the old B and B we checked into was one of the most haunted old houses in New Orleans. It was the star attraction for the many ghost tours in the area. There were old slave quarters in back of these old mansions. Many have been renovated, made into studios. We checked in and then snuck in the bird. We then left for the ten-minute walk to Jackson Square. We were supposed to hook up with my artist friend from Paris who I had not seen in forty years. By the time we got there I was in love. So many things to paint. All the buildings were really old and had beautiful gardens behind old walls. There were intricate wrought iron gates and fences. I passed by these really nice high-end galleries. They had topnotch work in there and I was really inspired. I felt that French Quarter was the capitol of the art world. In between the many galleries there were cafes and all types of street performers in colorful garb. The French Quarter was like a combination of Paris, Greenwich Village, Key West, and Haight-Ashbury.

    We arrived at Jackson Square. It was a big park with a black metal wrought fence around it. It was similar in size to Montmartre. All these different type of artists hung their work on this fence. There were plein air painters and there were abstract artists. There were many portrait artists. On one side facing the church there were fortunetellers. We met my friend from Paris. He was a portrait artist. That's what we did together in Paris. We had been arrested together at Montmartre during the police sweeps. We smoked homegrown weed in his apartment high on the hill overlooking the city. I met his friends who were painters. Like Montmartre, there were rules. You needed a permit. There was a waiting list to get one. You could still get away with painting plein air as long as you did not get in the way. We spent the first day just getting acclimated. The fun started when we went back to our room. The parrot was agitated like he was sensing some kind of invisible spirit there. We fell asleep right away. In the middle of the night we were both awakened by the sound of some knocking. I woke up about the same time as the bird and Fifi. The next thing we saw was a transparent image of a young black girl. She told us telepathically that she was a slave and she lived in back in the slave quarters.

    The next morning I met my friend from Paris and we painted plein air in front of this decaying mansion I was staying in. It was like Paris all over again. There were so many things to paint. My friend told me that New Orleans was a dangerous place. He said he had been mugged and robbed several times. He said that all his other artist friends had experienced the same thing. The French Quarter was safe but once you got outside it wasn't. Fifi was hanging with us when we were out painting. I sold a piece on the spot. When I painted outside I worked small because it was easier and quicker to finish. That night we were planning to go out and check out the music scene. In the course of a week I was painting at all the landmarks. I spent two days painting an old cemetery in the Mansion district. I spent a few days painting the oldest house in the French Quarter. It was a landmark. Originally it was Jean Lafitte's house. It was now a popular bar. Then I painted the old church at Jackson Square.

Then I began looking at apartments in the French Quarter and was thinking seriously about making the move.

The day after I got back to Palm Beach Gardens, I met a woman in a club on the island in Palm Beach. She was from Stuart in Martin County. That very day I went there for a visit and a tour. I decided to move there instead of New Orleans.

Stuart is only thirty miles north from where my parents live. The neighborhood where I live is called Port Salerno. It is on the water and there are a lot of commercial fishing docks. The Saint Lucie River empties into the Atlantic here. There are a lot of estuaries and off shoots of streams and water and marshland that make this area abundant in water and wild life. This estuary here is considered the most diverse estuary in North America. There are many bird rookeries on the small islands in the middle of the river. I have seen more varieties of birds around here than I have ever seen. It outdoes Aswan Egypt, which I thought held the world's record for abundant wildlife and flowers. Oyster beds abound as well. However, it still remains undiscovered and is known as an area where there is a lot of sports fishing.

Most yards have mango trees. June and July are heavenly during mango season. The air is abundant with the fragrance of mangos. I cook a lot with them and eat them at every meal. A lot of the houses in Port Salerno look like fishing cottages. Many of the houses remind me of some of the sections of Key West. The cottages all have yards and many have boats in their driveways.

FISH PAINTING, OIL ON CANVAS

The Manatee Pocket is what the water is called. In the winter many manatees will come up to the docks to say hello. At the turn of the century fishermen brought the manatees here from the Bahamas. They liked drinking fresh water. They were used to feed the workers. The manatees had a reputation of tasting good. They group together for warmth in shallow areas.

The Fish House Art Center is an old fish factory that is on the Manatee Pocket. In 1998 it was converted into art studios. When you are at its entrance, you walk through a tunnel which has art studios on either side. At the end of the tunnel is the water. In the fish house there is a tiki bar on the water. The docks start there and there is a marina. Boats are moored about one hundred yards off shore. Along the water there is a boardwalk which leads to a waterfront restaurant on one side and fishing docks on the other. The fishing docks are city owned and that's where the commercial fisherman keep their boats. They go out almost every day and usually bring back Spanish mackerel. At sunset the boats return and unload their fish on the docks.

Past the city-owned dock is another resort and marina called Pirates Cove. Across from the fish house is a do-it-yourself boatyard. Port Salerno has many other boatyards and marinas. The Fish House Art Center is walking distance to nine restaurants.

The name Port Salerno came about because, at the turn of the century a boat captain from this area was in Salerno, Italy. He thought that Salerno and his hometown looked a lot alike. Hence the name. Salerno, Italy, apparently has a lot of birds and fish.

Nightlife in Port Salerno is cool. There is live music playing at the different bars. It is known locally as being a rundown looking watering hole. It's a perfect place for an artist who likes to paint old Florida and fishing boats. It's truly an old fishing village. Many of the locals keep their pleasure boats here.

My studio, which opens on the boardwalk and marina, is the old icehouse. The space is a large room with three story ceilings. In the back is a kitchen. There are stairs going up to a second story loft where you'll find my bedroom and bathroom. On the second floor are holes in the ceiling where there used to be the ice shoots. There is a balcony and railing running across the second half of my space.

Port Salerno is a very natural and down to earth place. It's an area where there are more full-figured women than you would find in Paris or New York.

I had a twelve-foot Jon boat with a ten horsepower engine and kept it in front of my gallery along the boardwalk. I would take the boat out with my dog. We would putter past the sailboats moored off the gallery. We would head north past the next marina towards the direction of the inlet and ocean.

Our first landmark was Sandsprit Park, otherwise known as the "crossroads." That is where the Manatee Pocket ends and the Saint Lucy River begins. On the other side of the crossroads are several rookeries. A rookery is a bird sanctuary. These are small islands with beautiful beaches and coves. Hundreds of varieties of fish and wildlife abound. I would stop for a swim or take pictures to do paintings. Continuing on my next destination is the Hole in the Wall. Hole in the Wall is a small hidden inlet on the northern tip of Jupiter Island where Tiger Woods and Celine Dion live. The last six miles of northern Jupiter Island is an uninhabited wild life preserve.

My small boat makes its way through the inlet. This time a voluptuous woman that I met on the Internet was with me. We proceeded through this hidden entrance way. It opened into a small stream about twenty feet across. Hanging from the dense tropical vegetation were spider webs. Wild parrots, Roseate Spoonbills could be seen and heard. Going about a quarter mile further, the stream opened into a larger pond-like area. The solitude was divine, living as one with nature.

My date was beautifully plump with full lips in a constant smile. Her eyes were big and she had light, almost milky white skin. We bathed nude and sundried, stretching out on the boat. We got further relaxed by the joint of weed that she brought with her. It was like an acid trip without acid. She had a small dog too. We spent the rest of the afternoon there and then headed back towards the Manatee Pocket and the Fish House Art Center.

While here, I published a book about Florida Lighthouses. When I left the Keys I spent a lot of time traveling all over Florida painting lighthouses. In that quest I have driven over the entire state painting all twenty-eight lighthouses. I have seen all the nooks and crannies and surrounding islands this state has to offer. I discovered that Port Salerno in Martin County is the most beautiful area in all the state. Port Salerno is seventeen miles north of the Jupiter Lighthouse.

That site around the Jupiter lighthouse, which is only a few miles from here, has stories going back to 800 A.D. That was when the lighthouse site at the inlet was first inhabited. There were other stories that include armed conflicts with Indians and pirates to being a fort during the Civil War. And also being a site in the 1960's where a lot of smuggling had taken place. I painted and sold at least twenty different sized canvases.

The last seven miles of North Jupiter Island is uninhabited and is a large park. If you cross the inlet to Hutchinson Island that thirty-mile island was and is the location of some shipwrecks from the 1700's. Mel Fisher found some wrecks in the area. There are also wrecks in Vero Beach, which is not too far away.

I am watching CNN. There is a story on about the Middle East. Gaza Strip, the most populated place in

Memoirs of an Artist

the world, is under a blockade as to prevent terrorists from firing rockets into Israel. The story continues that there was a flotilla, which left from Turkey, of food and supplies. On board are many PLO protestors and others sympathetic to their cause. Even a few Jews and a Holocaust survivor are on board. An Israeli helicopter lowers a rope and young soldiers slide down to take control of the ship. Some people are killed and many are hurt. The world again is mad at Israel. Even some American Jews are against what the Israelis did next to stop the rockets; Israel invades Gaza to get rid of the bad guys. I still have mood swings when the price of oil rises. It even interrupts my flow about lighthouses.

In Pensacola I did a tour of the lighthouse. It was rumored to have a ghost that shows itself at a certain time of night. I stayed past closing time. When it was dark, an employee who I became friends with took me in clandestine and we saw the apparition of the lighthouse keeper's wife. Legend had it that the lighthouse keeper murdered her when she found him having sex with their oldest daughter. The Florida lighthouses on the panhandle are most beautiful. That area is referred to as the Redneck Riviera.

Sanibel Island was a fun place to work plein air. I especially liked Captiva, a small resort town on the other end of the island.

Many lighthouses are in remote areas. Some are on hard-to-get-to barrier islands. I self-published my book and I sold a few copies. I now can go around saying I am waiting for a check from my publishers. Of all the places I have visited in Florida, Martin County is the most beautiful.

Billy Selesnick

JUPITER LIGHTHOUSE

    I have been at the Fish House for a few years and have been happy and productive. I decided to go back to New Orleans for a painting trip. Lately I have been seeing another artist named Bean. People called her that because she was so skinny. Bean several nights a week just has ice cream for dinner. Bean paints plein air and moved here from Boston. I met her at a museum in the area. Bean and I made an all-night car trip. Actually when we arrived at 4:30 in the morning Mardi Gras was going on. We were beat and it was cold. We checked into our hotel in the French Quarter. It was nice being back without the parrot. Instead we had our two small dogs. We slept until noon and then walked to Jackson Square. My old friend was there as well as some new ones. Bean was also an art collector and wherever she went she bought art. Her house, although cluttered, was like an art museum. Bean went on a rampage and began buying art from everyone. It was a form of therapy for her. When we first met she began buying my work too.

Mardi Gras was going on and there were different events at different places. The colors at the parade inspired this black artist named Wesley who was with us to do a painting right there on the spot. It was amazing and Bean bought that one too. We were all going to go out later that night. Wesley warned us that people put things in your drinks and you have to be careful. That night a group of us went to this underground club right outside the French Quarter. It was a masked ball. There was an underground club scene in and around the French Quarter. Different nights it was in different places. Sometimes it could be in a house or private home, other times it could be in a warehouse. There were famous movie stars who were there but everyone had masks. There was no open sex, people were just smoking a lot of weed. I love New Orleans, especially the French Quarter, for its incredible subject matter and people.

In the beginning of October in 2012 I made friends with a sixty-one-year-old man named Travis, who sailed into our marina on his thirty-five-foot sailboat at the Manatee Pocket. He was previously staying at another marina under the bridge in Stuart. There was a big boating community there. There may have been some problems with the boaters who were paying fees to be moored at their docks. The ones who were freeloading may have been told to move on. So a crew of them on different boats all arrived on the same days. They were looking for greener pastures where they could live for less money.

Travis was from somewhere in Pennsylvania; He was a widower. He said when he lived in Pennsylvania he used to transport nuclear waste. He also had a blog online and was writing a book about all the people he met when he was sailing around on his sailboat. He was looking for work and I hired him to help me with some projects. He was holding out until his Social Security kicked in. Meanwhile he moored next to our marina. He came in by dingy everyday and took a bath in the sink at our tiki bar.

He plugged into the free electricity for his computer. He never ordered a cup of coffee at the tike bar let alone leave a tip. Such was the lifestyle of many of the boaters. He stayed in my gallery for a few days when I went to San Francisco to visit my son Jason. I was starting to get to know him.

One day Travis was late for work. I took my small row boat to check on him. I found him dead on his boat. He was slumped over in an awkward position – a distorted position, unnatural. It reminded you of a cubist painting, something Picasso would do. His figure was grey and distorted. He had a blank look on his face. His eyes were closed. His color already had changed to a bluish grey.

I raced back and got my landlord who was a retired emergency room doctor. We went back to the sailboat together in my twelve-foot jon boat. And my landlord said rigor mortis had already set in. The police were there in twenty minutes.

They stayed for a few hours filling out their reports. We brought Travis's boat to the docks and there it sits. Not a bad boat.

It was then I decided to write my memoirs on Paris. Seeing the dead body, triggered something in my memory. Slowly, little by little, my memories came back. I read George Jonas' book, *Vengeance*, over and over, and over again. That book is the story about the revenge of the Israelis on the PLO murderers of the

Israeli athletes in Munich. I was trying to compare what happened to me in Paris with the historical facts that the book offered.

It was if the shock of finding Travis triggered these memories that I always was so confused about.

I worked night and day for some three weeks reconstructing my timeline on what happened to me in Paris. Sustained by coffee and sweets I wrote all day and night. Tears of guilt and joy overflowed onto my pages. I heard voices. I was not sure if it was ESP or schizophrenia. I was in a manic state. The less I slept the wittier and more psychic I became. I spoke eight languages. I was literally having flashbacks from working at Montmartre. I was working with tourists from every country in the world. We all knew words in different languages. I found my friends were getting tired of me and only could take so much. I was talking non stop with them on what had happened to me in Paris.

I became obsessed with having contacts with my friends from the Mossad. I hired one private investigator burning through a lot of my money. I found private investigators online who claimed they could find people. I went to the office of one company and noticed a CIA plaque on the wall. I paid the required cash up front hoping to have contacts with my friends in Israel.

I began wild spending sprees leaving big tips in restaurants and buying luxury items. I was having a hard time sleeping. When I was driving I felt that I was being chased by the PLO. Every time I heard a loud noise I thought it was a gunshot or a bomb.

On the day of the completion of my first draft of this timeline I began to spin out of control.

I could not believe the memories that were coming back. The walls were closing in on me and I ran out of people to talk to in the wee hours of the morning. In a delirious state I called 911 on myself saying I needed someone to talk to. I also said that I knew where there was dead PLO from the 1970s. Later on I was led away in handcuffs and Baker Acted. The hotline operator that I was talking to when I called 911 also called the local police in Stuart. My medications no longer kept me in check. The death of Travis and my memories of Paris, were too much for me to process.

Being locked up really was a relief and I was diagnosed with post-traumatic stress and bi-polar disorder. I was in a straight jacket and handcuffs.

I spent two nights in county lockup. It is called New Horizons. I met some interesting people there. It was just like *One Flew Over the Cuckoo Nest.*

My first day in the hospital, in order to cope, I began doing portraits of the patients and attendees. I showed them to the psychiatrist to prove to him I was lucid. Then I started doing yoga classes. Some of the patients joined me.

I have heard that finding dead bodies does something to the neurons in your brain. The psychiatrist seemed to believe my story of Paris and the Mossad. The psychiatrist let me out on my third day.

I had my melt down that Steve warned me about so many years before. I had my epiphany Yael and others said would happen to me.

Recovery was just three months of processing what happened. One friend said I made the whole thing up to feel more important. He advised me not to pursue my story. It would just get me in trouble.

My father, who believed me, says I have an important story to tell.

I still get road rage when I am driving and every time somebody honks the horn I feel like I am in a war zone and bombs are going off.

The secrets I have left have to do with the question, how many people did I hurt? I am not talking about a few sexual affairs I had that I did not mention in this book. I mean people who could have got hurt as a result of me participating in these operations. I can't remember. My amnesia was too much like Jason Bourne, a character in a series of espionage books who due to brainwashing could not remember what he did. I think it's been such a shock, opening Pandora's Box. Maybe this story should have that name.

LOCAL LANDSCAPE

I still make a modest living selling paintings. I barter a lot. If I need to go to the doctor, a painting usually pays a bill or two. By this point I have been doing two paintings a week for many years. That almost puts me in the category of my idol Gustav Moreau, the symbolist who painted eight thousand paintings in his career. Even an idiot after painting so much would have to improve. My works have made it into collections from Paris to Rio, New York and beyond. I feel I finally have a right to call myself an artist and maybe even a part-time spy. I am in a monogamous relationship with Bean. She accepts everything about me and lets me paint fleshy women. She also helps me with my book.

Benjamin Netanyahu is prime minister of the State of Israel and will soon be putting together a new government after winning re-election. I am still obsessed with the Middle East. I still keep CNN on twenty- four hours a day.

Luckily I have multiple interests to bury myself in. All in all, I am more whole now. I am still very passionate about my painting and took another trip to New Orleans. Lately I get inspiration from the waterway and ocean.

I still love to paint and get a lot of satisfaction from it. I think I processed or come to term with all those memories.

The End

Thank you for reading.
Please review this book. Reviews help others find Absolutely Amazing eBooks and inspire us to keep providing these marvelous tales.

If you would like to be put on our email list to receive updates on new releases, contests, and promotions, please go to AbsolutelyAmazingEbooks.com and sign up.

About the Author

Billy Selesnick was born July 18, 1951 in Trenton, NJ. He developed an interest in art at a young age.

Billy was very affected by the events that took place during the Sixties, Civil Rights movements, Flower Children, Vietnam protests, and Woodstock to name a few.

In the late sixties, Billy started attending several art schools because he decided that he wanted to spend his life painting.

In the early seventies Billy moved to Woodstock NY and continued to paint. It was then that he enrolled in Goddard College in Plainfield, VT and partook in an independent study program.

In 1974 Billy was accepted in Goddard's European Masters Program. He left for Paris to participate in a two and one half year art program. It was in Paris where Billy had some of his most memorable experiences.

Upon returning to the States Billy opened his own gallery in New Hope, Pennsylvania.

It was there that Billy gained notoriety and received many commissions for his art.

He also travelled extensively around the world, painting in many countries. He would return to New Hope as that was his home.

In 2000 Billy moved to Key West, Florida. He lived there for seven years and completed hundreds of paintings.

In 2007 Billy then moved to Palm Beach County where he continued painting. At that time he decided to write about the experiences he had over the years of being an artist, travelling the worlds and being a parent to three boys.

ABSOLUTELY AMAZING eBOOKS

AbsolutelyAmazingEbooks.com
or AA-eBooks.com

www.ingramcontent.com/pod-product-compliance
Lightning Source LLC
Chambersburg PA
CBHW050346170426
43200CB00009BA/1757